A WIDOW'S WINDOW

HOPE NWAKWESI

A WIDOW'S WINDOW
Copyright © 2020 Hope Nwakwesi
First Published in Nigeria 2016
Revised edition 2020

ISBN: 9798842061501

Hope Ifeyinwa Nwakwesi
+234 8080251984

Printed by Unusual Publishers & Printers Co.
Tel: 08023303114, 08033069833
E-mail: unusualpublishers@gmail.c

CONTENTS

DEDICATION

I dedicate this book to every woman whose status changed the day her window was broken by the death of her "his" and all their children. It is an end YET a BEGINNING; you can make it right again.

ACKNOWLEDGMENT

I give my greatest thanks to God in whom there is no variable and to whom I have my HOPE for years to come. But for God... To all my fellow widows who shared their stories with me, we wear the same "shoes" though different in sizes and steps yet our path is the same.

To all my families and friends in the religious and social circles; I say thanks; you have either given me JOY as a lubricant or STRENGTH as armour in all your treatments.

To my Publishers, thank you. Your support in affirmation that this book is a need did strengthen my zeal.

To my loving children Ifeoma, Kenechukwu, Ijeoma and Chioma, thank you for your support in this journey. You all are the best of all I have.

FOREWORD

Prior to reading through Sister Hope Nwakwesi's book, I had claimed abundant knowledge in the plights and ordeals of widows, because I was raised by a widow. My mother had been widowed after barely three years of marrying my father, I was about two years old and mama was pregnant with my only full blooded sister. I experienced firsthand what Sister Hope describes as "the tears of pain and anguish that come with his death" the undignified actions and abuses meted to widows in my native land because of our unfriendly and ungodly cultural beliefs and practices.

Now I know that my knowledge is actually limited in the light of the strange and staggering revelations contained in this book. Strange still to me is the fact that the same ordeal and difficulties experienced by my mother over fifty years ago are still prevalent in our clime even in this 21st century. I have known Sister Hope as a consistent, diligent and prayerful Christian, one of our Bible Study Group members in our former Parish ANCOPEN, VGC, Lagos, a dependable ally in the work of evangelism and missions to which we were devoted.

But until reading through this book, I never knew she possessed such a vibrant literary ability as a writer, a poet, and a composer. The book you are about to read will not only open your eyes to the ordeals, the deeds and the needs of widows but it will as well teach every reader that life is ephemeral and fragile. No one sets out to become a widow but the reality is that it is appointed to man once to die (Heb.9:27), what is uncertain however is when, how and where.

The death of a married man certainly produces a widow and according to the author, a "WINDOW" and a "HOOD" these attract a lot of peeping Toms and uninvited guests, many with untoward intentions. Widowhood produces hardship and calls for necessary elixir, succour and support. It makes most affected women and their children vulnerable. Society should therefore assist to supply the needed succour and soothing balms to the inner and invisible wounds inflicted by the "HOOD" instead of adding salt to the already painful wound.

Sister Hope the poet has employed a lot of simile and metaphor and other idiomatic expressions to drive home the points of what widows are passing through such as alienation, suspicion, assumptions and presumptions, telling us that they are indeed uncalled for because widows are human beings who are entitled to their own social space and economic engagements particularly now that " two has now become one".

Reading through this book, one would definitely learn a lot of new vocabulary and even some hitherto familiar words and acronyms that have acquired new meanings due to the ingenuity of Sister Hope the poet and wordsmith. Such words as Hood, Corset, ABU, and the likes will add to the reader's wealth of knowledge. The author has some golden advice and wise counsel for widows and non-widows alike.

Women are advised to develop a keen interest in the affairs of their husbands so in case of the unexpected
they will not be strangers in their own land and thus be swindled out of their legitimate inheritance. They are also advised to be engaged in meaningful ventures or regular employment before and after the Hood as work helps occupy the heart and reduce emotional trauma in times of grief.

Relatives are also advised to consider widows and their children as fellow human beings and allow them to get over their difficult moments before the struggle for property left behind by the deceased. It is good, reasonable and biblical for widows to remarry if they find it impossible to cope with the resultant loneliness of the Hood and this they should do prayerfully and early enough before it becomes too late.

The book contains a lot of sermons suitable not only for widows but for everyone, the need for salvation of the soul, dependability on God and His word, which is described as "blackmailing God", accepting the sufficiency of the all sufficient God and prayer, prayer and prayer.

Lastly, I wish to state that readers will learn to appreciate the plight of the children affected by the hood and how they too can assist their mothers to achieve quick recovery and swift reintegration into the larger world in their new status.

Beloved, I recommend this book not only for widows or widowers but to all because it qualifies as an academic, moral, spiritual and general study book, it elevates integrity in seemingly disadvantaged
positions and doggedness in the face of undeserved oppression. May the good Lord bless us all and intervene in the affairs of our lives so that this hood will be deferred to old age when people can
be better placed to cope. Amen.

The Rt. Revd. Olajide Adebayo
Diocese of Igbomina West (Anglican Communion)
PASSIONTIDE 2016

INTRODUCTION

At his death, placed on me is a covering beyond the physical. As other hood walk around without identification, so do our hood stands out with its segregation.

THE WIDOW AND THE HOOD

This is not just a book. It is a vista into the lives and times of "The Widow" whose change in status as a woman arose, upon the death of her husband. In certain cultures, her present state carries a stigma of abandonment and it is treated in different ways by different people in the society. She can be seen to be loved by all but beheld by none. Her agony is only fully appreciated by her God and her innermost self. She is most times a woman in utter distress especially in her inside. I write this book with a desire to share the tale and perceptions of others along the path of widowhood.

This I believe will not only help you see through the window; but will show you the real "hood" in widowhood. It is what I call the in-close in the CORSET of the hood. Tied by the society, she is shaped by all as desired, mentally and physically. Why we ask and how they ask? I write this in the belief that it will not only help you see and act accordingly by showing you the in-close in the hood of a widow but will also help fellow sisters in my tribe to understand that they are not alone in this race. We are all wearing and walking with the same shoe, though our sizes and steps are different but the path on which we tread is the same. You are not the worst nor the best. Just understand that though situations do change, yet God never as his promises are ever the same. He is truly the same yesterday, today and forever.

All He desires of us is to encourage and support one another. Let it be told to you that amid that beautiful smile lay a similar grieving pain of loneliness and fear with its shame in a fall. I have it even if you can't see it; the journey has not been easy for the past twenty five years. I simply handed my entire steps over to God and embraced with gratitude what his grace and mercy brings on my stairs. The hope in overcoming was grown from the solace of his endless love more than any human love. Stand strong, be confident; the dark cloud shall surely go away, it always does as long as you are determined in dexterity; a completely new dawn must arise. What you want and what you give in to it will decide the brightness of its glory.

Weeping may endure for the night, but joy comes in the morning. (Psalm 30: 5).The sun must shine after the dark night for a morning must come. The day is still shining, don't wait for it in the darkness to come to you; walk to it and experience the joy of its rays. Your dreams didn't die, your aspirations are still alive, yes his loss is a pause but there's a phase which he handed over because he believes you can. Your joy can never be wiped off in the tears nor can it be destroyed in those pains. It is only your fears that are drowning them. You are the only life guard that can save the 'you'; take hold of the 'you in self' and move gradually to the brightness of the new moon. As life has all the weather, the rain, the summer/dry season, autumn/ harmattan and winter, each with means of enjoying it, so do situations of it. Find a purpose in your future and take the steps of departure from the past; a lot more joy awaits you at the arrival. The time it takes us to arise and move though differs, but it is until you decide and begin the move for it to happen; the sooner the best. The table of widowhood revolves on a pivot and touches everybody in its way, the ripple effect of it which we have often failed to accept is enormous. The color of life of a widow is painted with "the beauty" and "the beast". "The beauty" being her God and the "beast" is the Hood she is made to wear on her personality.

As I watch the world look into my life as a widow; an open window as it seems, they look in constantly yet act as blindfolded. As an artist exhibits his paintings a widow is exhibited at the gallery of life. Because all the evidence chosen by most around as seen in their cultural mind, are her plights; very few are interested in its purchase even when she is most beautifully painted. Alone, becomes a life best to her soul as society places a tag of invisibility on her; she feels it on their looks, she smells it in the air; seeing the brightness even in the darkness. This is because without her knowing the art has been painted in her sub consciousness by the culture as a tape programmed on replay, with her heart wearing the pain so hidden in her smiles. Her world though hidden it seems, can be perceived from within rather than imagined on the outward appearance. To most, your imagination which you mirror into her world, is born either out of pretense, wickedness, ignorance or pity; while to the few supporters, theirs are out of genuine love born on empathy that grew from within. Whatever your reason, look into her eyes and from thy inner sight find compassion, to view the window of her world. Most likely then can you truly appreciate her state. For there, is the point of contact that can motivate you as you decide what you will do to her. Whether you will enhance her well-being or add to the pains and aches she has to live by reason of her status in the society. The intricate life of a woman is more overwhelming in widowhood. She battles daily in pain as she's seen from the eyes of "who is she" even pleasure. This is what most have failed to or pretended not to see in their imagination of a widow's world as they place her in an "invisible calamity".

Fortunately, this life has become my book of choice which I invite you to read, though you may feel it's unfortunate. I say otherwise, because the two sure components of life are birth and death. Even in our dexterity it is destiny that completes; yet the cultural expectations and assumptions say different as they make the widow a villain and her dead husband the victim. A widow rides all day alone, hoping all will feel the wind of the wheel, experienced every minute in each her circle of influence and provide not just a support but an action that will eliminate every act of exclusion. To everyone in her world what is required most in your feeling of sympathy is to give out your treatment with compassion. A proverb says "If you go to the market and throw a stone, you may be hitting a relation". We must remember that widowhood is in the life cycle of every woman once you are married and the food you are thinking it is another person's portion might turn yours someday. We need to get involved to see that every part of its ingredient is well prepared peradventure it becomes your meal. Don't be so inhumane, do not be a murderer. Your ill action can add to her pain and in depression lead to her early death.

Be assured that if empathy is shown to her to lighten her burden, her hope will be restored. If a glimpse of hope is seen on her steps her pains are smoothen. And for each small balm felt her grief is reduced. In the tiniest experience of these she's strengthens to confront her journey; with less fear and more courage eliminating every act of shame on her path. This helps her in conquering the one difficult battle of keeping our home intact with dignity and sanity as both her family remain with her. It is often said that the issue in life is not so much the destination but the journey. Widowhood is all about the journey not his death. The death is an end; a destination known already but widowhood is the journey; the beginning of another experience. The expectation of every female in marriage life is to become a wife and a mother with every other desire as a female. But in his death the cultural and societal expectations, exploitation and the struggles to survive presents another path for her the become part of the journey. In it all, it's how well we handle the trials we encounter on its pathway that determines how we get to our end. It's not the destination that gives us the test but the journey. Every one of these tests produces a result; negative or positive.

Are you an obstacle or a launch pad for the widow along your path? You can be an encourager rather than an abuser to her. Plead a widow's cause, Isaiah 1; 17e. Nothing in her carved into grave at his burial except her status as his wife with the love from him, which is the physical as I can attain the spiritual love of a late husband is a force that keeps the widow with her kids. As a widow, the Hood is the challenges we meet along the way, the unexpected twists and turns, the disappointments we fight to overcome from families, friends and foes. The expected assumptions we've made a belief that covers our personality, the silent voice of our screams and the loudest shout of the society's silence are the journey of widowhood. Is it complicated; or it sounds simple? They are not as simple as we feel but not too complicated to undo. It is a battle of being able to overlook all the incomprehensible, disheartening and disappointing products of our culture under which most people sees a foothold to release their venom as they decide to develop a new product of compassion in the spirit of love for human rights

The roadmap of a widow to emotional stability cannot even be likened to the deadly lonely part of a battlefield. This is because the widow's enemies are often unknown to her. They masquerade in various forms and characters; some as friends, others as relatives and colleagues. You will never know who your enemies are as the same troupes who are on your side may turn around and fight against you unexpectedly especially with the permission of culture.

Being widowed, you most times feel insecure and vulnerable in the life context as you become the man with a hip in a patriarchal society where ability are defined by sex as against competence; strength as against sense. Nevertheless, there should be no quitting of this sortie; one will and should continue to strive in action to occupy until emancipation is achieved. This we must do by taking every act of debilitation as conquests with positive attitude. You must continue to forge ahead, keeping your gaze focused on the Creator to create a path that will lead to the cap waiting to be worn in victory by you tomorrow. You must always look to the upwards towards your victory that brightens and never down to your loss; it's drowning. With a positive gaze you are strengthened to stand. When you look down to the expectation of your position you are bent to be broken. Being positioned up right will bring out the resilience that is inherent, which will not only strengthen but empowers you with the outward zeal of a positive attitude that gives you a greater physical and supernatural energy to move on in this life journey no matter the circumstances as you are reminded always God's promise; The thief comes only to steal, kill and destroy; I have come that you have life, and have it more abundantly. (John 10:10)

A WIDOW'S CREED
We beg not your sympathy,
Only pray she thy empathy.
I ask not her provisions,
Only seek me, thou support.
We demand not your acceptance,
Solely thy understanding we solicit,
I appreciate your distance

Make us not an outcast
Close thou thy eyes
Imagine I in you
as she in her;
How treat thee in both?
Just that she ask,

much too many you feel,
Do not exactly same
Just a similar
Little understanding
tiny support
Not too far a distance
Plays thy empathy
a welcome compassion
That show an exit
Away then goes
thy reel of OUTCAST

CHAPTER ONE
A WIDOW'S WORLD

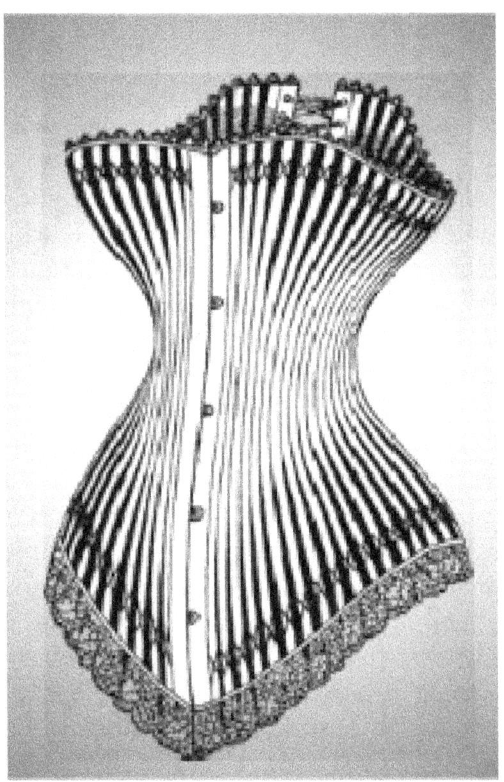

In Close In Corset

*Once his death, you are tied out of sight by all with
their thoughts, attitude, expectations and your
emotions. Until you loose yourself in God will their
strings cut to your freedom.*

When the vision to write this book finally overwhelmed my resistance and procrastination, as I started, one word that I desperately wanted to point out was the unwholesome treatment and feeling of OUTCAST, which evolved out of my personal experiences. Though it was so heavy in my heart, yet I had some doubts. Wanting to be sure it was not just my imagination, I started asking other widows of their experiences and stories. I realized that same word was common to all of us. It was expressed directly by some as "treatment as an outcast" while others had such to which they refer to it as "the alienation" and some explain it as "segregation" and "rejection". Some in portraying it went out of breath as they were short of words, not knowing exactly what to call it. No wonder the various titles "sin of omissions, invisible calamity, the Secluded, Victimized, Shunned etc. The treatment I tell you abounds all round to justify the titles. Widows are made to experience and suffer different extent of deprivation and discrimination in the society.

From culture, families, spiritual and secular communities depending on the countries and cultures where they belong, there abounds a share in all tribes with some culture having the most form of it. The problem with being a widow in our society is what I could only describe as being in the *"in-close in CORSETS"*. It is not just fighting to cut the cord of the string tightrope of expectations but also the Hood to which you must wear in their descriptions. And I ask, since the Hood does not make the Monk, why should the Hood be used to define the widow. Widowhood is one of those silent pains in life and would have remained so if the society can take away their own pain. Today in most of our African societies the widow is trapped in the cultural practices and rites that have designed her exclusion. There's this grown mental culture which has an assumption of what women in widowhood should be. The expectations being nothing more; anything outside of that grows a more reality to their suspicions. It is the Hood to which a woman on the death of her husband must wear around in her subconscious like a dress in her struggle, to which the society has no issue in adding more as long as it defines loss.

It creates a hole to which most has no problem digging further. It's a perfect realization to her in-close in that Hood that confirms her acceptance to most. Losing a husband is a process that one will either allow to dominate or must work hard at subduing it in moving on. But I must say, it is better and easier as a widow to work with prayers to subdue it because you can never put an end to the challenges until death. Even if status changes again as one remarries; the scar never goes and the ability of enjoying the pages of chapter two is learning to read chapter one without opening its page. One must as a widow imbibe the inner strength to persevere and surmount the life's challenges which get added to her once the status changes from "married" to " widowed" with that "something inside so strong". It's finding oneself before he became the pages of your book and relearning self without erasing him because any attempt to bury oneself or him present a delusional soul in an illusion path.

The life of a young widow starts with an arduous path as she is segregated from the society. The difficulties in this journey are often caused by lack of understanding and supports even from your fellow women that often time alienate you. A widow automatically becomes a sex toy in the mind of most as she loses her status of a "family friend" because you are not defined in a family context. The nuclear and extended definition of family father, mother, children and father, mother, children, aunts and uncles separates you, as you float like oil in water not just in the definition but in their acceptance. While to most women you are a burden, a duty to get rid of, to a lot of men you are a duty to be carried out their will. And a few men who genuinely may want to stand up to your support most often shy away to avoid societal and family gossips arising from assumptions and expectations. With the perception of widows, the word gossips are indeed alien only to a widow's imagination because she has to live with it.

Misinterpretations and gossips are part of her life irrespective of the genuineness of her actions, because she's defined most by her sexuality. Exposed to this helplessness and vulnerability as she is tied out of sight as desired by all, she struggles to scale through the peeping eyes and wagging tongues of the society often forgotten as she loses herself in search of the financial "need-only" assumption for widows; only to discover later that loneliness is the absolute poverty in widowhood. Like a snail we all go back into our shells, as relatives, friends and others through actions and words label us an outcast. The definition of widows provides a label of difference that breeds shame hiding her voice. Often as a result of this labeling that has become the hood, most widows naturally withdraw at the onset more to protect herself from future abuse as she contends with the obvious. A widow and her society have both in their conscious and unconscious, culturally grown a concept that a joyous and exuberant widow might be seen and said to be enjoying the husband's death.

Our various Africa culture stated it in black and white; you must display a double sobering spirit even if you have to fake it, especially to be seen mourning your husband in all family and friends setting. The society in its culture deliberately or otherwise destroys your confidence in living a normal and complete life at his death. In all the widowhood rites the main aim was to make you less attractive and confident as if your life ends at his death. Though in our society today, as a widow you can escape the rites but if you don't work to take back your life and take charge of your rights; no matter how low the level to which life reduces you in the Hood, some people will still want you to vanish and never be seen talk less of being heard. To them you should exist in a world of invisibility, seen only to the eyes as a vapor. The reason why various title of widowhood article that goes from "Sin of Omission, Invisible Calamity, the Excluded, Stigmatized and the Shunned is because widows are seen as an object without any innate appreciation as defined by patriarchal system.

As a young widow, I remember having to deal with a relation of mine who was begging me to make the job of helping me easier by coming to their home because of his wife. I affirmatively told him that "I am a pretty woman; I do not want anyone feeling I have come to take over her husband. It is the children that need the love and assistance most, send your driver with whatever you want to give them or ask him to come pick them up or I drop them whenever you want, I will gladly release them". The invisible existence to which they place a woman in the hood provides and promotes an avenue for humiliation. They want to ridicule you as much as possible as they fight to subdue you. I had a family friend who abandoned us for years and on meeting him accidentally one day. In his apologies he said "I had to stay away because I did not want to abuse you". Really? He disappeared after burial, no phone calls or checkout in five years yet we are in same city? To men that give excuses of keeping away because of the weakness of the flesh, noble men, I call them!

However, how many times do they send greetings and gift items to the bereaved family of their so called brother, cousin or best friend? The good ones make it a point of duty to put smiles on the faces, joy to the hearts and love in the souls of their widowed family and friends with care and cash as possible as can without making the women come crawling in need. These needs remain the cash and care with none being more important to the other. Our needs include that of belonging and recognition. Turning her to deposit bank can as well be as damaging as placing her in a dormant position. To those that see us as a burden, I say, a widow may be deprived of husband, finance and love of her man, but she is still a human being with God given abilities to cater for her home and children irrespective of the seemingly tough circumstances.

The greatest gift you can give her is your love and respect which must come from your compassionate being. Remember that God in his goodness gives his sun and rain to the just and unjust and never loads anyone with a burden he or she can't bear (1 Cor. 10:13) as such has the power to change every one of her statuses. "I ask not her provisions". All that a widow seeks is your support and with God on her side she will fly above the billows of life to the best possible. I remember being removed from a duty I had executed so well by a new executive director who does not believe in the ability of a woman. He said it to my face that he won't allow me to do the job again because I am a woman and that he will only give it to a man. Globally the term "woman" has its own disadvantage amongst men but adding that title "widow" I tell you make it worse.

The in-close in CORSET of widowhood makes the situation more challenging and demeaning. You are string out of sight in size and season by family and friends. In our society I tell you, being a girl is tough, being a woman is tougher but being a widow is the toughest. I have concurred that in this journey the men folk obviously enclose you to keep you under their control and for their use; however, the womenfolk do same in their rivalry and insecurity. We should always remember that death is a destination of every life at birth, and in a married life widowhood is path we will walk though at different time. While some will escape it, most won't. Let's show some kind of empathy; even if it means doing nothing, though apathy is an abuse, it is better than humiliating a woman that is going through pain for no fault of hers with degrading treatment. But the most compassionate act of empowerment that is universal is that we work together to stop every act that violates women in widowhood in our society.

To we women, let's change the act, it is never a rule. It is a practice turned into law to which we have determined to use as rule even as it is ruining us. We are sisters. A sister like a sheep, is helpless but as sisters are "help-full". Let us build a sturdy bridge that can hold our generation of sisters strong as they walk that path that is inevitable of any woman to falls in love to marriage. And as widows, one can help by letting all as much as possible know the damage done to our person. The silence has remained the veil on widowhood. Our culture of secrecy the oat, a bond that seems binding to evil. When we take every act of humiliation without complaining or confrontation, it is termed acceptance and as such nurtures the growth as it continues downward to generations. A woman does not mean less nor her submission meaning slave. Her status as a widow should also not be translated to an outcast or handicap. It is only a psychological change that will improve with time, which happens faster if she is supported and encouraged by the society. She will do her best to stand better when they untie the string to which they have shaped her. But in their refusal, as a widow, you work to untie every of their strings to beat the odds of their actions.

Tonia narrating her painful experience said "I have had friends and relatives in positions of authority that could assist me by giving me jobs to execute. I run a procurement business that is doing well and with a good profile yet they will not patronize me. I watch them in pain making others rich while expecting me to come begging them for money all the time. Why? Asked Tonia. I know. It is to keep you in an intermittent need, not that they give freely when you go seeking. They simply enjoy the humiliation to which they subject your helpless person as they use that to build their ego and satisfy their desire. The pain on our faces is their joy, but whatever it m y be, I advise widows NOT to let anyone abuse them any further. If anyone is in a position to provide work opportunity but refuses, don't go seeking for alms from them because in doing that we are giving them more room for abuse. I have learned to streamline such people; you cannot continue to give them that satisfaction of rejoicing in your pain. Let's give them a dose of their drug; turn away from them and never to return again. Put do it without bitterness. Face front your helper, for there is always one for every season that comes and watch them come back in shame later as they watch your victory. "Only seek me, thou Support" says our widow's creed.

I appreciate more, the people who created work opportunities for me then, because from there I have both the physical and psychological needs satisfied. Creating such opportunities empowers you further, as it is said, "give a man a fish, you feed him for the day, but give him a hook you've feed him for life." A widow's blessings we pray should be more of an avenue to make her create her own wealth than being giving alms. Alms breed laziness and promotes abuses. The ability of the society and government to provide structures and facilities for widow's empowerment will help eliminate the human rights abuse that exists for women in the journey of widowhood. One of the greatest ways of dealing with emotional pain is by working. It keeps the body and mind physically and emotionally busy, thereby giving less or no time to thinking and grieving. As Eric Fred said "work is an effective means to deal with the anguish of death and void." The death of one's husband creates the greatest void and anguish which needs to be filled. A full work to live in walk with God remains the sure remedies, because the exhaustion that comes at the end of the day after exerting all the energy and the grace felt in the love of

God helps in sleeping better. The worst period of time as a widow is the night of sleeplessness.

I can tell you from experience that the less busy you are, the more you cry and lament because you spend that time and energy thinking and analyzing your state in the solitude of your bedroom bored. This increases your anguish as the void turns your life into a dark hole of loneliness. To the women who have termed her as 'sex tool', I always ask these questions will she be the dog you have assumed her to be if her husband were to be alive or if you were to lose your husband, will you love to become the dog you've made to be? The death of her husband creates an emotional door that is not just a sex club. Her choices and taste was not buried with him. So when next you think through her libido do a complete comparative analysis. 'Close your eyes, Imagine I in you as she in her". How treat thee in both? Just that asks.

To the men who see in a widow an object for their libido and fantasy, I say don't be a man that must intimidate a woman in need. Every woman is someone's wife, sister, daughter or mother and being widowed does not wipe away entirely those positions. Close the eyes of your outward man to see through the inward being. Will you be happy if such treatment was given to any one of yours? The status of a woman in the Hood should not be identified by the size of her hips. This symbol when presented for your appraisal or assistance as most men do is the reason why most family and friend find it difficult to support her for financial and social freedom. How can you criticize and condemn another man of rape while that is exactly what you do? By subduing the vulnerable widow to your 'will' before you can assist her is an emotional rape. Her 'No' never became 'Yes' when she succumbed, her 'Need' overpower her 'Will' as she allowed you to rape her without force. Don't be quick to say it is without force. Just because there was no physical struggle doesn't make it consensual. You forced her Will with her need to which she fought with you in your conscience. Her fear of survival consumed her pride and in grief she swallowed her shame as she took the pain without its feeling. The tears in her soul shed the blood of her womanhood. The experience of that moment will continue to be a part in her path that keeps her in tears as she curses the act. The effect of such curse I really believe does not equal the ecstasy of the few minutes of fantasy and ego feeding.

A widow said to me, "After the death of my husband I was caught up financially and could not pay our rent. The landlord threatened to throw us out. After my constant appeal of time as I continue to gather money from my 'petty trading business'. Caught between relocating and the acquired debt on rent as I plan moving out, the landlord promised a waver in exchange for sex". He was so happy with his conquest that he offered further free rent for her stay to continue. Well, in your rejoicing, know that your trap caught a helpless prey and when you are tempted to take that seemingly advantage, it is a disadvantage to destruction. Help her as we save our lives, sternly withhold your help and let her go if you can't be a tool in God's hand. I am somebody's mother, she was someone's wife, and we are peoples' daughters and someone's sisters. The earth will continue to revolve so is every experience, do unto others as you will like them to do to you or your own. Whatever the case may be, in my opinion, walk away from humiliation of any man as he is probably not the one God wants to use to support you. Speak out; don't be cut up in pride and shame. Most importantly find widows around you to share your journey. There's always a mentor waiting out there to help you mold your life back without shredding further your being.

The Beast

It is the untold humiliation that widows have to contain within widowhood that is the beast. The stories of these abuses are often the same. I remember walking into a friend some years ago after a long time, a distinguished member of the senate to ask for a job under his authority. On our meeting he acted so nice, he asked of my children and how I have been coping. He showed so much concern as he appreciated God's work in my life so far. Finally in gladness born out of his warm reception, I presented my request. The spirit was moving in my favour, my prayers were answered I thought to myself as he immediately without problem made every arrangement for me as he called the director in charge of procurement. After speaking with him, I was sent to his office and my company was immediately allocated a slot. The degree of my excitement was out of this world. To me, my time has come, I continue in my thoughts as my face radiates in hope. I could have purchased my dream house on mortgage but for my quick return to inform him how it went and to express my gratitude to him so far. With appreciation I told him I had to rush back to my city for an emergency regarding my kids in school. "No" he said abruptly, "you are not going back today let me bang you." Not truly understanding what he said, I answered "what"? He said it the second time, still not sure what he meant I repeated "what"?

Just as my common sense was registering what I thought he meant, he landed with direct word "you are not going today, let me fuck you". Like a thunderbolt striking my brain I screamed "What! Just like that He proudly replied "if you want to my driver take you to the house and you wait, after all I don't beg women". Oh my God, I was consumed with mixed emotions. I paused a second, looked at the beast, for truly he was a short fat ugly and classless beast. I was torn between anger and shame; feeling so humiliated I picked my bag and left. As I left the place that day, I was struck down with a very high fever. I do not know which was stronger, the shock of his insult or shame. But whichever, they both must have mixed with the tension of my children issues in school to give me that shiver that broke down my immunity as I began running temperature immediately. I tell you it wasn't easy because the devil was busy showing me the millions worth of the contract I was about to get. But I thank God for His Words and promises that strengthened my Will and cleared my doubt, making it possible for me to overcome by walking away completely without looking back.

All I did when I realized from a source that he had cancelled my name from the job was to pray and move on. Though the incident traumatized me as the sound of his words and the picture of his audacity with the insult stayed glued to my memory for a very long time. Yet it didn't deter me from continuing to search. The psychological impact in time goes into the subconscious only to resurface at the slightest provocation. Till date, I still can't remember it without a quiver and some degree of anger. I remember, I kept telling myself that the job was not meant for me as God's blessings will not have sorrow added to it according to His Word in Proverbs 10:22; especially when the pain and gain began a battle of the Titans inside me. The responsibilities of widowhood was so high on me as my bills continue to stare me in the eyes yet the humiliation and pain of that assault and the sorrow of its shame were worth my letting it go. However, though my company was removed but I tell you, all the approved contracts awarded during that period that mine was removed, were cancelled as new government came into power. Was it my prayer answered? No! I never prayed for such. Yes I did have a prayer that affected the Distinguished Senator that was answered, but this was God's reaffirmation that His blessings He adds no sorrow. I would have lost both ways, my dignity and the contract's assumed worth.

I almost didn't blame him as I walked out that day; after all I had ignored him for years and coming this time he must have taken it to be that I was desperate to be looking for him. That is one way the devil uses to keep one in shame. It makes you believe that it is your fault. No, it is not! I was not looking for anything in his groin. I had a seed; I wanted a fertile land to plant so that God can water it for me. Remember God said He will bless the work of our hands. That land for sure was not it as I realized later. Our fertile land will never attack our dignity in tilling rather our strength. God told Adam that by the sweat of his forehead he will till the ground to eat, so being the Adam in your home as a widow; what we should lose in our planting is our physical energy and not our emotions or self-worth. What a widow want most when she comes to you is to get work not to be fiddled, as most assume.
The assumptions that she's free and lonely though not farfetched doesn't mean she has become a dog, for even dog have time they work. When she comes to work, making it an avenue of exploitation is dehumanizing.

As a young widow, my advice is don't make yourself a charity case, begging without purpose makes you an object for abuse. It is not by polishing your appearance seductively, you should have content at all times but never neglect the container. Let it always be your additional portfolio not the main. Though, in all this your effort, you will still meet obstacles; but in that you, should boldly tell yourself that you have the ability and favor of God to overcome. To most widows, the trials are such that one can never be able to say it all. In each path, the thorns and stumps scattered along the way is such that one must learn to walk through without its scare as you will be wounded by one or the other. The cultural practices and rites across our culture with widowhood have placed a stigma on widows that remains the basis of most actions she receives; to even the ones she exhibits. They are the result of so many mental culture of "omission" we've developed over time.

I went to the birthday celebration of a family friend few years after my husband's death. As expected everyone was happy and dancing. It was a merry mood to which I joined the dance floor. In between the interlude of rest and discussion I realize that my friend's husband who had been staring at me was lost more on their expectation than the lust I assumed when he said to us in a conversation that I cannot remember the genesis, that if he dies, no man will marry his wife as he wouldn't want it. Taken aback in anger, with a cynical smile I warned him to be sure never to die because there is nothing he can do about that. Of course, my joy was dampened as I withdrew from the celebration. I obviously was not expected to be happy not to talk of dancing. I was in a girlfriend's house party alone trying to live but he looking into my world in his imagination aroused the worst, my sexuality, who is she sleeping? That's all that comes to their mind once you're seen radiating.

His mental calculation was only on my sexual needs. He forget the responsibility of raising four young kids to which he and his wife are struggling hard on. Couldn't he have imagined the pain and the suffering I must be going through and relate it in empathy to the wife? No, to him and most people, I should be in the state of anguish, otherwise I am being screwed by another man which I am not to enjoy but I am, hence the gladness. Have you ever seen a woman dressed in black or white mourning attire dancing and singing joyously not even in a church talk less of a social gathering? Mourning is personal and the idea of induced or enforced grief is an aftermath of our practices and rites. If a widow in a moment of relief takes to the dancing floor there will certainly be another woman to remind her that she is not supposed to do so especially as a young widow after all your husband is dead and every feeling of joy in you should be dead.

If I cannot dance years after my husband's death with a large percentage of the gathered persons thinking I shouldn't be doing so if I were not having fun with the widowhood. Is it in mourning attire will I be able to do so? I tell you that will be totally unacceptable and shocking to all around including me. Yes, me because we have been indoctrinated to take it to be an acceptable norm. Grieving a loved one is natural, personal and cannot be manipulated, not momentary joy and excitement are God's gracious act of therapy. Marriage is a bond; I think that a bond cannot truly be broken either as widowed or divorced even when done the emotional entanglement is like a colour mixture, once mixed cannot be separated. It can only be adjusted or improved. As a widow, all she's doing is adjusting. We are only working to improving our life with the best we have not forgetting but forgoing while formatting the journey anew. One must learn to find a definition to the status. A widow to me is a married 'husbandless' wife with fatherless children. The complexities of its definition are less to the complication of her life. The search of a place of understanding of who to be in a patriarchal society where women's social and economic acceptance is largely tied to a "Mr" becomes another ignites of anguish. Even in her world she falls apart as the Ms, Mrs and Miss frowns at her meddling in their title and space.

Men Created in True Image of God
There are indeed honorable men who are really portraying the image of God and are true to their consciences. We each have someone whom God keeps close to our hearts in prayers and practices. There is one to whom I will forever be thankful because he genuinely allowed God to use him as one of those who made my load lighter. I remember after being introduced to him through an in-law, he took genuine sympathy. In one of those occasions, he gave me a business that got even my in-law astonished. I remember my in-law asking me on showing him the job order, "what did he say to you?" I replied, nothing. You mean he did not ask you to sleep with him or return some money to him? I said no because truly nothing close to that happened.

All through my years of doing jobs under his leadership nobody believed that he was just doing what he could to give me an opportunity to create resources for my home. As I made sure I did the jobs to the best of my ability as specified so as not to disappoint him. How can his generation not see the favors of God! It is highly impossible, for God will remember his labor of love. Yet, despite all these, you could see his extreme carefulness in most of his actions as he was subconsciously alienating because of that general attitude. I remember one of his colleagues removing my name from a job I was qualified to execute and when I went to plead with the colleague, he said to me in the most sultry and derogatory "do you want to be eating both ways? I guess my facial response prompted the second response "You should continue only with his" meaning his colleague.

That was their imagination and stories. It best not to be disheartened, no matter the obstacles, be sure at all times that those men who can understand your plight with God's true Spirit for support do exist. They allow the love of God to supersede their lust of flesh in providing a loving support as capable. But these persons must have to be courageous in their good deed because of the persecutions they will encounter. They are going to be faced with accusations and possible stigmatization which can discourage or make them withdraw from their good deeds. In journeying through, the situation most times can be such that you become the Israelites as you stand between the Egyptians and the Red Sea, you feel so helpless and confused yet burning in anger and pain. But keep your pace in peace, God parted the Red Sea for the Israelites to pass, as Moses prayed. He will blow the storms away, in each place of despondency a helper is right there for you. Whoever it is, must come at God's own time. You will never know when and where but in God's best time and at his planned place his help will surface. Don't be a social nuisance; be dependent on your God's ability more than man's capability. Move on if an assistance wants to turn to slavery, be rest assured that your children will never starve to death or go without clothes and shelter, he feeds the ravens, (Luke 12:24) and clothes the grass (Matthew 6:30) much more his wife and children, he promised to be to us.

There is a help angel for each of us and for those guardian angels, let's continue to pray and protect them every time with adequate understanding of their awkward position. I tell you, at her husband's burial, in the drops of those tears were the dowry returned not just to the husbands but to all men by our God. In so doing he took us in as his wife breaking all the covenant of our marriage and instituting his greatest covenants with his promises of an everlasting kindness in mercy. This He keeps, even after He opens another chapter. He gives peace to our children, filling our days with signs and wonders, for how can you explain your daily survival? You've got to believe it yourself that no matter the assembly of persecutors, they shall all be condemned in your victory. So work till your victory becomes their shame. God has instituted a covenant of peace with a promise that we will for sure forget every reproach of widowhood. (Isaiah 54). The shame of each of their act is a sign of his wonders to come. If a "man" in his help is heading to shame get out and go forward for it is not in him but of God that helps come.

Two days after my husband's death as I got into our home in the village, in the midst of all that was going on around me, the shock, confusion, fear and the pain wrapped in an unimaginable anguish as I grieve the life ahead, came a man I do not know. He never introduced himself, at least none that I can remember, I have never met him before and never seen him thereafter; I cannot even remember his face only that he was a man. Standing and looking down at me in sympathy, he said to me "ndo in my igbo language meaning 'sorry' that is 'my sympathy'. Get your Bible and read "Isaiah 54" and hold it to your heart that it will all come to pass". As I responded helplessly nodding my head, I assumed then it must be the painful feeling that has obviously overwhelmed my desolate soul to glaring eyes of all; that he was talking to me about. But today as I remember it and in looking back I can truly say he must have meant both the feeling of that day and the words of those scripture. Every bit of it has come to pass in my life and that of so many other widows. He takes over from our husbands and becomes one with a difference. With him there is no "till death do us part", it becomes a relationship of love to eternity, faithful to the end, though not an engagement ring as He welcomes a new season of another chapter for us whenever love knocks on your door again.

CHAPTER TWO

A WIDOW'S WINDOW

Joy is fountain of feel experienced
when you live in hood as your
soul encounters peace with
the faith that all is and will be well.

A WIDOW'S WINDOW

Open my world,
once his death.
Fully dressed, yet naked;
As Words to shame,
deeds to fear
All abound
Though Sadness and joy,
Are constant in conflict
Resign not to grieve.
Even in pain
Lone the feel,
abundance he loves,
His grace our hope,
with comfort his fills.
Rejoice for in all,
Your solace come victory.

"As a teenager I always fantasized about that right man, who will be the love of my life, my confidant, my friend, my companion, my husband," said Tessie. "Coming from a Christian home and having the conviction of no sex before marriage, I had no boyfriend till I met my husband". Like she said, they got married and within four years she became a mother of two children, expecting the third one only to wake up one day barely 25 years of age, to be crowned with this title of a widow.

The window is like a human's heart. A window that is opened to allow sunshine and freshness into our homes to refresh our lives allows pests and dust to come in. So also is the human heart the window to his or her soul; it is opened to receive both love that will brighten and refresh his or her life and pains that will threaten and grieve the soul. But unlike the house that we can easily clean the dust and kill the pest, dealing with love and grief of the heart is far more complicated. For a woman, she finds love in her man; married with hope of togetherness. And with joy from day one, she takes her vows including "till death do us part". In her feelings of excitement make it impossible to imagine or try to understand the excruciating pain that comes with the reality of that verse of the marriage vows. If a priest or marriage registrar were ever to pause in a marriage ceremony to explain it, I believe no bride can ever articulate the weight neither will it stop any woman from saying the desired long awaited response "I do". The secret things belong to God, (Deut. 29:29), thank God for that because the cases of unmarried adults would have negated the biblical expectation of a man leaving his parents and finding a wife, both living together as husband and wife to procreate. (Gen 2:24)

The marriage, as sunlight starts with all brightness and HOPE to the future with her man. The arrival of children further enlarges the dream. In unionism of marriage, working hard and praying expectantly daily for the best every new morning as the up turns and down curves of marriage are being tackled. In all joy with occasional sadness with all gladness believing in a brighter and better tomorrow for, and in all cases, she process her dream which she has built in his. Be it the teenage girl or woman raised in an African culture, the journey to marriage to most is more often an economic and social security than the fantasy of Romeo and Juliet; but certainly never a Delilah and Samson fancy like. So as the patriarchal society changes you as a baton from father to husband's authority and security; like clothe when your father gives you away in marriage; he pulls off his, allowing your husband to put on his. Adorned in that dress; you shine only to the society, that often no matter the extent of your ability, all your effort and strength should be under his cloak. You're identified only his design as you either succumb or is subdued to walk in his path dressed as his plan. The reality of it is that in his goodness you grow to glue in that plan as you either trash or plant your plan in his; making it "the plan". Then comes that fateful day when that door is opened and here comes the news that pushes all her walls apart. And when this unplanned happens, every dream and hope is scattered and her world becomes a tale of a horrendous disaster varying more in decree than in inexistence.

His death is a rip off of his dress presenting an "unplanned". The plan that they have developed is altered and she is thrown into a world of greater confusion, and that becomes an opening which keeps her "fully
Dressed, yet naked". In abstract, she processes her flight unable to fathom where she will start. As if the shredded emotion and broken dreams are not bad enough, the society immediately encloses her in a frame of their ideas of the "widow" that makes recovery more difficult to which so many have succumbed without recovery. I call it the "In-close in corset". Unfortunately, these ideas are not complementary and their severity depends on where she comes from and in whose company she functions. X-rayed by these ideas, it becomes difficult for her to puzzle back the shattered pieces of her life.

The journey starts with break of the news; it hits the brain with a big bang which goes straight to her heart, shattering both the physical and emotional walls of her life. Her soul is immediately opened to the five most dreadful emotions of fear, pain, grief, shame which graduate into loneliness. The effects of these emotions can be consuming to which the society in the name of culture expands further as you go through rites that are so emotional debilitating. Rosie said; "when my husband died, I was made to go through rigorous cultural exercise. While I have to contain the countless meetings and questioning at odd hours of the night and the sitting position designed for me. After his burial I was told my hair will be shaved. I was asked to shave my pubic hair while they shaved my head. I was made to eat from everything that can burn as everything I touched was termed unclean. I didn't like it but, was told I will be ostracized if I did not go through it and won't be allowed to come bury my aged father when he dies".

The fear arising from this confusion initially exposes the widow to a world of real uncertainty; especially in our part of the world where the culture is yet to embrace or support the issue of remarriage as they present you as unclean in their rites and practices. As she struggles to survive, in recovering, all effort to puzzle back the pieces of her world, she finds her window cannot be fastened as the world takes the sized latch giving her an undersized one. With this as a widow she will either continue in a struggle to fasten it or she move her focus away from the window as she face the door for her recovery, ignoring the peeping eyes. At the news of the death of the husband, his woman's life takes a dramatic turn. She automatically wears a crown crafted in fear, decorated by pain, to which the world in joy colors with shame and fixing it on grief as the title "widow" is bestowed to her. Removing the 'n' did not change the application because like a window are you structured in the wall of the world as you wear your crown. The crown is accepted by our patriarchal system that violates women's dignity.

Though this crown can never be likened to crown of thorns on our Lord Jesus Christ on the cross but has a negative disposition similar to it, as it places the widow in a state of absolute loneliness. Having been presented accursed, she walks down the lane of life alone as others ride through her path with little or no respect to her presence. With the news and their actions she cries for her life and acts for her children. In crying she is wailing. While in her act she fights to keep up a fair condition to save the children despite her all-consuming grief. My daughter did not like it continued Rosie. She protested. "Mommy, you cannot allow them treat you like this, what's wrong with you mommy, why are you taking all these". I didn't like it, I wasn't enjoying it but I had to do it because it is our culture. My fellow women I turned to, said; "you have to do it, it is our culture". It is a storm with dry rain as nothing can be seen capable of wetting your life to lubricate a pure joy in that sadness, yet for the kids she stays painless in the most excruciating process of life being strong outward yet shattered inward.

The Storm

The life of a widow can be likened to a storm. During the ministry of Jesus, in one of those preaching moments, he entered a boat with his disciples and asked that they cross to the other side. As they were sailing, Jesus was sleeping at the rear of the boat and they were confronted by a raging storm. Yet Jesus was still sleeping that his disciples had to wake him up and immediately he woke up and calmed the storm. (Mark 4:35-40). This is the story of widowhood experience that women must understand. He commanded that a man should leave his father and mother, take a wife and they become one and also instructed that it is till death separate them. We are His products. He knows the life span of His products but have no expiry date on us. His warning of "time to be born" though it's there, but the passion of love and joy of life makes it impossible to think of death in marriage except in old age.

He called the wife a helper and gave us 'him' a covering in a blissful marriage, and then he allowed him to die. He took her covering, the plan, her crown of glory, in our society where her economic and social acceptance is dependent on him. He stripped us naked in a culture that is yet to stop blaming women of his death as defined in all rites. Where was God when this storm was building up, Sleeping? This can be likened to His sleep at the back of the boat. The storms of hood at his death become boisterous and intimidating with the family consciously or unconsciously blaming you as the society tends to look away. But what else can you do other than to wake God up. We must learn to count upon him to do what he did to the stormy Sea by getting up to live with the I can. This as a widow you must do to overcome by looking away from the bad situation as you position yourself to God's goodness to restore calm to the sea of your life. In the stormy life of a widow, it is only God that can abate it with his sweet warmth in love and the sunshine of his hope. Once you welcome the light in the obvious dark tunnel he will make all things bright and beautiful again. He can and will calm the storm, it is only faith and work that is requires from us. The effect of this turbulent storm of widowhood isn't just painful, it is sure excruciating. Seeing any good out of such a painful experience and inheritance requires all the discernment you can muster, both from within you and what you can glean from mentors. The greatest mentor we need as widow is God's Word and a fellow widow. It is in God's spiritual guidance and other widow's mentoring that we can get everything required in navigating through the flood of the hood.

The news first starts as a story that seems like a dream; even if the man had been sick for some time. Ada whose husband was sick for over six years said that the day he finally gave up the ghost, it was like a dream to her. It took her time to realize the reality of the situation as she moved initially from the imagination of being in dream hoping to wake up, to that of the thought that he has gone to hospital and will come back soon as before, talk less that he died unexpectedly and suddenly. I really cannot remember when I stopped looking into every white 504 Peugeot to know if that was my husband in it, even after watching him being laid to his grave in our far away country home. It is a dream from which we prefer not to awake for fear of its reality, yet we are not asleep. It is a dream that you are often forced to wake by your family and friends as members of his family start scavenging for his property or the abandonment of family and friends slaps so hard on the face that it gives you no luxury of lingering in the what if and what was. The reality of her states often forces her alertness to which many has termed a celebration as gets up sooner working like a robot with no feeling of emotion.

THE JOURNEY OF NO RETURN

It is only in losing a husband can a woman understand in depth the real meaning of two will become one. He is gone forever with something you will never get back. May we never embark on a journey of "no return"! This was my Reverend's favorite prayer. I never identified the full impact of it till after the death of my husband. This prayer oscillated in my spirit for years even after he was transferred out of our parish in the church I was attending then only to realize that it was one of his important prayer points as he continued to pray it same way when he came back after many years. I must have been the only one that fathomed this prayer for real. Though death is inevitable, it is a prayer that every one of us should add in our daily prayer for all its worth. The power of religion to healing I realize is more effective only when one is in search of restoration not miracle. Being restored is having an inner filling defined by one's faith in God that manifest the abundance of content as we humbly avail our ears to advice.

I remain very grateful to a good friend of mine for her noble deed because my life would have remained more in regrets. I remember that because I did not want my husband to take the journey he never returned, when he asked me to give him the money at my disposal I refused. Being a weekend and the banks were not as efficient as of today, he went to a friend who, though had the money, but came to me to know why I was refusing to give him. Understanding my reason on the issue then, she implored me to give him the money as he took my act of refusal to be lack of love and support of his career. I obliged, for which I am thankful to God. In my search of what I could have done to avert his death comes a quivering wreck as I ask myself; what if I had not and he had that as his last thought? My grief obviously would have been beyond imagination. And I implore every woman, if ever your husband is travelling leave complain and make sure you are at peace with him because the "goodbye" might really be the "bye-ever". My husband's death is indeed a journey of no return; as I have never been able to stop winning back in check. We should therefore endeavor to disagree in love in our marriage because that is going to be our memory to anchor on. To hang the weight of those feelings is better balanced on smiles of each memory rather than regrets.

When my husband left home on that fateful day he left instructions and assignments of what should be done before he came back and those I should leave for him as he promised he will complete once he was back. When we bid him "Goodbye", waving back he left, less than a distance down the road he beckon on my son who ran down to him, what they discussed I do not know till date, he hugged him as we watched. Waving again, he turned and walked away as my son ran back. Never did it cross our minds that that was indeed the "bye" that will be forever. A picture of that day remains vivid in my memory that even a hundred years from now, as an artist I will draw a picture perfect life portrait of that scene to all details. A position of sadness filled with a feeling of reassurance of hope in love at the last experience can help in healing the wound. By the third day he was to arrive, we were all prepared for his arrival assuming that his journey was delayed as it usually was at that time. Telephone communication was not readily available like now so there was no anxiety of broken communication. We believed he was on his way down from the east. The journey must have been delayed, a common occurrence with road journey in Nigeria. We prepared and waited that day, but little did we know that he was already in the mortuary because he died the previous night. The bond in marriage is sacred, two shall become one.

When we look deep into most things that happen in life we can't help but continue to thank God for the powers he kept solely to himself because of the wickedness of human beings. I realized later the next day at the break of the news of my husband's death that his spirit did visit our home that night. I remember vividly that I was awakened by a sharp stab towards my heart, very painful, as I sat up looking round and wondering, I had nothing to make out of it. While sitting up and couldn't sleep, I heard some noise coming from my children's room, as I got up and walked in, I saw my sister sitting up on the bed with my children tossing around in their sleep restlessly. It was a very restless and sleepless night for us all. We got up all tired at the break of dawn; lazily I dragged off to work after sending the children to school. I remember my colleagues teasing me of being pregnant as I was very moody, lying around the office table and did practically nothing that day.

On getting back home later that day, we waited unsuspecting for his return until about 7pm when that knock on my door came introducing the visit of an in-law and his wife, uncommon though, but not unusual. As we welcomed their coming, by telling him that his cousin travelled. They sat down and started this story with the two sentences I can never forget among the tales of that fateful day. "There has been an accident, your husband was involved." In panic I asked looking at him, "where is he?" Their look to each other made me ask further "is he dead?" Their faces confirmed the yes that their mouths never said. In shock, like lightning I was pushed out of my house, frightened almost to death. At first the only emotion I had was fear as a result of the shock from the news. The force of that shock I tell you was so incredible because how I got up to a two-storey building on a dilapidated staircase remains a mystery to me till date. A staircase I never climbed because of the bad state of the steps. An in-law of mine who was living there would have a heart attack if I ever give such bang and scream today on his doorstep. The bang and scream I gave on his door shook the building. As he opened his door, I was terribly shaking with my heart panting as he opened the door, frightened almost to death, as I told him what I just heard. The few minutes it has taken him to recover and stabilize himself from the shock he got from the sad news had disorganized my family because we came out they were all scattered running to all directions, looking and wondering but not knowing which way I had gone as the speed with which I ran out unsettled them as they did not expect such reaction. The emotional state of losing a loved one should be best imagined than experienced.

CHAPTER THREE
A WIDOW'S JOURNEY

The worst of one's fears, pain, abuses, and deed of shame can never be forgotten neither can it be undone but they can be put in a good use in a new life we find ourselves or decide to take. Though it all leaves a negative feeling, process your emotions on the positive; ignoring the actions of people who have no fear of God or respect for your emotions. This, you can achieve once you honor and acknowledge God presence in every circumstances, in that you'll grow with a deeper understanding and acceptance to the situation as you realize there is nothing else to you which eliminates the fear as it reduces the pain. As you will find out that all you need is the respect and humility of heart to all people at all times and in all things.

Tosin said, "As I set out to marry, though we had different religions and upbringing we had love which I believed that with our values we will make the marriage our own. My husband though an extremely responsible man, a great provider to his family, a doting father and a loving husband, however was not able to stand up to his extended family or put his foot down on matters relating to his own home affairs as regards to the interference of my in laws. This resulted in them having a say in virtually all matters relating to us which cost me so much at his demise. It was a Sunday, after the activities of the day, as we retired to prepare for the new week, at about 8pm, he left home to pick up some medication from a pharmacy in the neighborhood and that was the last I saw of him. I waited, but at about 1am and yet no sign of him I began to panic. There were no mobile phones at the time, so I could not reach him neither could I drive out at that time and to where if I could. At about 5am, I left home in the company of a security man and drove to his parents' home to check if there was any sign of him, from there to his friend's place and on began the search. By daylight, I alerted a few more friends and we set out as search parties in different directions. From one morgue to another, one police station to another. We went round the city until we came face to face with the reality of his death as we found his body in the trunk of our car abandoned on the expressway with gunshot wound in his head. The fear of accepting my fate cannot be explained. That day marked a turning point in my life, ten years of marriage, 33 years of age, three children between the ages of nine and three years old and with a pregnancy, behold am a widow. It was never part of my plan, so I had nothing to do or say but to watch, the shock sent me into a limbo. My husband being a Muslim, he was buried within two days even before I could recover from the shock of the news."

This must have been tougher because when it happens, you have to first recover from the shock of news to transcend to the fear of the situation by coming face to face with his corpse as the pain and grief take over which can take days to a week to process. The immediate burial I think must be a harder one as you want to recover from the shock to experience the burial for a more appreciable memory of the last moment. Thank God for he is the greatest healer, in time he heals all wounds.

Like in a marathon, the sound of the gunshot kicks off the race, so it is for a widow. Once the news is broken, the story begins the journey. Tonia said, "As daybreak the next day my home was a beehive of people. Thank God for our

African culture and the Church. People were coming around to encourage me and keep me company" When this happens, we are surrounded by so many people, true sympathizers and mockers, the true sympathizers came with words of comfort and assistance of all sorts, they do not only appeal to you in comfort to stop weeping, they keep your mind busy by striking all kinds of funny conversation, while sitting around you. There is this "psychology agreement" that make one sitting beside a "newly" bereaved widow to pray for another person to come before she leaves. Newly, I say, because that's how long the contract as you will one day wish the clock be rewound in the days of loneliness and feeling of abandonment. The mockers you know may not say or act it directly but they come to know if you are crying enough or to know if you are happy that your husband is dead; while to some you are either celebrating the wealth or the freedom. They can analyze how well or deeply you are grieving for all who cares to know. I tell anyone I go to condole on losing their husband to hold their tears if they can, never mind if people will think or say you are not crying enough and that you are happy of your husband's death. I always say to people whenever I hear such comment that God will do the same for them so that they can cry or rejoice better and win the crown. Be assured that your cry is not there and then, it is 'after and when'; a continuous process that even in the days of joy and celebration you will cry not just the tears of joy but that of sorrow, hoping he was there to rejoice with you or even praise you for all your effort.

The strength of all widows begins with the comfort of those visits. They really helped and we are all ever grateful for them. That is an aspect of our culture that we should continue to uphold. In fear, confusion and despair I wailed groaning like I cannot describe, praying and wishing seriously to wake up to see that it was not happening to me. Why me? The wrong but one question we ask most. If not you who will you will or wish it to, my mother will always ask. The pain of a widow can be deep rooted; I truly learnt the real meaning of the word "excruciating" in that experience, not even a tranquilizer could ease it off. I remember a doctor colleague of my husband that came the next day, she was shocked at my frightened sight as my eyes were popped out red with all frightful emotions oozing out from my pulse, sweating and shivering at the same time. She must have been so concerned with the loud pounding of my heart which she didn't need a stethoscope to perceive. She sent for some drugs with which I was injected. She came back hours later surprised that not only was I not sleeping but that I had not slept at all since then.

As all these confusions were taking place internally you have to be strong within and for the children while taking care of issue of his burial externally. I thank God for my in laws because they truly never added the cost and confusion involved with preparation of the burial to me. They did it all totally, only brought me in places where I must be with no added cost to me. Most widows from their stories, in that pain had to take care of their husband's burial, both the cost and confusion with even in-laws, relations and friends swindling them at will, for a young widow that is truly stunning. Ese said; "Then came the burial. Believing that I was a small girl, I was not consulted in any way concerning the burial of my husband. My in-laws took care of everything both in decision and implementation all with my husband`s resources to the last penny. Apart from the available money they used as desired my brother-in-law even demanded for the money he said he added for the burial which I was made to pay back to him later". If you were going to use her money she should have been involved to know how best to utilize her money, after all she is best to know their purse.

Her Emotion

The fear;
Her heart dismayed.
Our will in fright
As fear abound
In thought and deed,
Imagined though most
Often yet experienced
Aggrieved to heart
In soul engraved
Memories of scars
God our Will;
Overcome we will.

According to Bose, when I said "I do" over thirty years ago, it was on the joy of being cared for by her man like every other woman. At such an early age, still a student, becoming a wife and a mother almost immediately, things were getting better as dreams were developing into reality. Everything was very peaceful and beautiful with the interlude drama of every marriage as expected of two different people coming together. I still proudly tell people that I had a wonderful man, with the authority of a head, and the meekness of a devoted servant who showed me tender care. He truly understood headship as a man and the weakness of a woman. The best short ten years of bliss that cannot be equaled nor forgotten. He took total care and responsibilities of the home, though not a saint but he cannot be faulted on the smallest duty. For my husband, you can never and dare not come near his children and wife. A complete father and husband. That actually helped my accepting to his death truly as 'fate'. This is because, I know he would have fought it through, had it been physical or were he privileged to see it coming. The love and joyful desire to continue to take up his responsibility would have caused him to secrete the greatest adrenaline to give him enough strength to bulldoze even the greatest mountain. I did not blame my four year old daughter when she asked me "mummy why didn't daddy fight or beg those people".

The arm of death is as strong as life itself and indeed a debt we all must pay, when and how we do not know. Our only prayer should be that of being in love with our creator and his created to earn an eternal place in peace with him at home in death. When bereavement happens, the 'if, why and how' are too many, you cannot understand any. One must first destroy these questions in order to move on or else they will destroy you. These questions stampede our emotions. This explains why some women, during the first few weeks of getting the news are simply mopping with undefined emotion. It is that of shock and confusion. These 'if, why, how' and questions unanswered keep them in a state of forlorn that their only wish is to wake up from an assumed dream. They do wake up after sometime to the reality which still confirms the fact that "I am a widow" a new title bestowed in her new status. The only way to kill these questions before they kill you is to align and agree entirely with that Igbo name 'Chima' meaning 'God knows'. It's a name that became more meaningful when I came face on with Widowhood. When you become convinced that God knows what has happened and what he will do, then can you be able to regain your spirit for survival.

I do believe that the devil is fighting seriously for supremacy here on earth, but I have come to agree totally that when God is not in watch the watchman watches in vain (Psalm 127: 1). God is in watch over all his creation, it is him that allowed it, nothing he does not permit happens. I may never understand it; we cannot question him and even when I did, there was never a desirable answer. If we try to rationalize it, it makes no sense. All we can do is to resign to his Will in faith. Like a child, believe sheepishly on God's promise that remains the only and absolute solution that can unleash the strings of the corset in the hood. Likewise if his family can believe in the power of God's ability, so will they be able to hold the family of their brother with love as they comfort and console each other in their loss. They must empower their fainted heart by looking forward in hope to conquer rather than drowning and wallowing in pain with fear, dismay and dislike, losing more than a member but a whole family.

At his death, the pain of all is consumed, as his wife and kids grief the loss of a dad and husband so is the parents and siblings grieving for a son and brother. The issues shouldn't be whose pain is more but an understanding that everyone is dealing with some pain. Little wonder why the Bible recognized the widow's mite? It is because God knows the magnitude of each person's input. What can be said she lost in her giving is at the least commensurate to the rich gift of the other member. Depending on how you perceive the other, the family of a dead man nuclear and extended is in a loss and analysis of who lost more becomes the genesis of war which benefits no one in the entirety. A loss is heavy, and the weight of its pain is relative. While the loss of a dollar seems small to the rich son walking down the street, it means life to the pauper's daughter right across in the same road. Understanding is the road to recovery that binds the bereaved family in love. The assumptions in widowhood are the number one source of fear. Everyone concerned must work to overcome the fear with a hopeful attitude especially the widow. I came across that saying that Fear is means "False Evidence Appearing Real", I used to think I believed in the saying, but in losing my husband, this meaning for sure became false at first. How can anyone tell a young widow like me with little children that all the bleak future she is seeing with hopelessness and helplessness is false and that there is no evidence to it? The saying however remains true with time when you allow God in faith to take over. When you stop blaming and expecting, and start believing and understanding; you realize that the bleak future with all the seeming attributes and attitudes are pictures the Devil brings to deceive and destroy us. God alone who knows the end before it began, makes true the meaning in our lives by providing all the help with real evidence of his plan to restore the hope in a next plan that brings the victory.

The Pain
The news a dagger
Stabs through to heart
Deep it pierces
A hole to my soul
Held in awe as I watch
sharpened by each pain
For Over in all it looks
Seemingly Permanent
As weakness engulfs
Difficult the heal
Eases in time the feel
To build a peace
Where hope is home
With springs on joy
As His Promise to fill
Is full with love
Breaking a yoke

To a glow of his glory
That wipes away
The pain of our parting.

It is said that time heals, sure it does but a widow can heal in time without living healed. True healing in time is all about feeding our faith by starving all fear. It is about refusing to grieve no matter the pain. It is not easy, you can never comprehend it all; but when those circumstances overwhelm you and you are surrounded by all doubts. When all friends exclude you and you are completely striped off. When all efforts looks like nothing good can ever come your way, look beyond your situation by focusing on the initial expectation you had as a wife with a husband in the family. Find the girl in you that had that dream that attracted him to you. Remember your dreams before your togetherness and your desired destination. Look at each stage of your life as you had it in your imagination. Build the castle in your imagination and move into it anytime you feel low and alone. Keep your imagination in a nation you'll love and then nurture your moment in its future. The beauty of it helps you to keep the family destiny focused to the destination as it fuels your faith to move on in spite of the obstacles.

In this, you learn and master how to move from the situation to the station. I learnt in time that power of keeping one's faith high to your future no matter how impossible it may appear at the present, trusting that God will send help to take me to the desired destination. The mastery of this act helps in time to heal and live with healing and not just exist in healing. To live with healing is the faith in taking the bull by the horn as you struggle it through looking for how to land as against letting it throw to where you land. A potent faith gives you an escape from the pain that abound all around the Hood. It strengthens your ability to take decisions that one feel can move her forward irrespective of all contradictions. In it I mastered in time when disheartened and scared to "Do it Afraid" Joyce Meyer. She is so right. Don't let fear limit or destroy you. As a widow the feeling of pain are like the potholes and stud litter around the path. The danger being that you can hardly take a step in your journey without encountering one. In all circumstances; you will either be physically or emotionally aghast by the attitude of most people especially trusted ones.

In the journey of a widow's life, the fear is going to come in different forms, from that of shelter of a man's cover, to being abused when in need, as well as that of questions from the kids and many others from you. The pain of often not having a clue of what next can be like an ulcer sore. But whatever it is, it is best to build ones strength in the spirit; find the Word and hold to it. There is a God's Word at every turn, look out and listen hard. It is so subtle right in the inside, normally hidden from the volatile audience. Make your spirit your guide. Whenever your spirit is keyed to a decision and all that is impeding you is fear as you wish he was around to give his opinion. He's right inside urging you on; all you must do is to overcome it by leaving all doubts and step into action. The pain of widowhood is delayed longer with our position to dwell in the past either so that he will not be forgotten or we will not be seen to have forgotten. We deny happiness in believe of question; can one be truly happy again? To which we've taken an answer of No, in comparison to when we have mastered our marriage foregoing when we were learning to know how to master it. It is the right of everyone to be happy, because God has great happiness for all His creatures even in our painful moment.

So, you should think most for you and the children, not the people or their expectations. In loss of husband, a widow develops all sorts of fear especially thanatophobia "fear of death" and atychiphobia "fear of failure". The fear of dying and leaving her kids creates a reserved seat of pain in her within. But in the fear of failing one often limits oneself as she becomes more dependent accepting painful abuses that naturally cut into the psychological well-being. I have come to realize that in the journey of life, a spirit inspired decision isn't a risk because when it is taken, it yields any or all of these three results; (a) the desired result, (b) the door to an opportunity for the result or (c) an opportunity to other door with a better result. Remember in your loneliness, we have a husband who is in the spirit; one of his ways of communicating with us is through our spirit, so destroy the fear by keying inward to your spirit.

The spirit is willing but the flesh is weak (Mark 14.38). To Strengthen your Will pull out the spirit in an action. The strength of the spirit is stronger than the weakness of the flesh to which we most often fall.
Irrespective of the state of any marriage, the shock of a widow especially in the case of that journey of no return is better imagined than experienced. In all the counselling in marriage and your planning at the home nothing can ever prepare you for what you will experience in that situation. That reminds me of a friend who came to work one day with bruises on her neck. On asking her what happened, she said; "I will never break the news to a woman that just lost the husband". A brother- in-law of hers was shot dead and on getting to the wife, as sympathizers were gathering outside they realized that they had to break the news and no one was brave enough. She decided to do it. In breaking the news, unknowingly and unexpectedly the woman in shock screamed and jump to her neck grabbing her shirt, it took the intervention of men that ran into the room to free her hands off her neck as she was almost choked.

The strength of that shock is as fast and strong if not more than a lightening; it can be very fierce, hot and frightful. It is difficult to say for sure what a widow's first reaction can be at the break of the news. The common feeling is shock which produces an unimaginable fear especially to young widows. According to Ese whose husband died far away in the USA, her first blow was receiving the news of her husband's death through a direct telephone call by the husband's younger brother. "I almost slumped to the ground if not for the support of people around because I was in a public place". I tell you, such a person is a murderer, and it shows how much he hated the brother as to want his children to be orphaned overnight, because that woman could have ran into an on-coming vehicle. Thank God for people around that came to her rescue.

Back to my story which is our story; it looked like a dream initially, I believed that I was sleeping and having a bad dream and will soon wake to reality. With time, I did wake up to reality but not to my old person of being an Eve to my Adam but that of a new person, a widow, a member of Naomi, Ruth and Orpah society. When this happens, at first your physical and spiritual sight goes blank, you cannot see any silver lining at the end of that tunnel because for sure in that tunnel there seems to be no end in sight. As the reality of the story begins to unfold with no glory to behold, the pain and its grief take over magnifying the fear and with the shock diminishing, the feeling of shame begins to creep in with one asking "why me, what did I not do right?" It is the time even the most faithful spirit filled Christian has to continually affirm herself in words on God's faithfulness as doubts are more in thought and feeling.

What can be more than this asked Stella? We all thought so that day we received a new name in a new life. It horrifying. You are either not crying enough to soothe your soul or you cannot cry at all as your soul goes in shock. With these emotions and the more she has to protect her children, especially when they are too young. You must put yourself together to face them as their fear now is focused on you. They watch your actions and emotions in fear and as a watchdog, look on to you watching you as hawk, while in solitude they grieve their fright. Your strength to stay strong is their power to absorb their pain as they process their fears. The children in their grieving display different attitudes; some are strong, some are weak but no matter the portrayed emotion, they are scared of what may happen to mummy and them. I remember my four year old daughter one day pleading with me barely three months after my husband's death, she said; "mommy please don't let anything happen to you, I don't want you to die, I don't want to be an orphan. It was shocking to hear her say the word "orphan" rightly wondering how she understood the true meaning and import of the word. Like most children who cannot grieve with crying she was so deep, always on her own thinking that I had to keep a close eye on her in order to distract her thoughts most of the time.

Her emotional fear which I realize was torn between why daddy didn't escape the death and that of being an orphan if mommy dies was an issue that drew her into a sad poet; that I destroyed ignorantly especially when her school principal commented on how she was always writing sad deep poems even for school programs. The woman must hide her own fear in order to encourage the children. She must drown her own emotion to contain the children's own. Even with the adult children the widow also has to control most of her fear so as not to overburden their emotion. Her load is heavy both ways, and the best you can do is show some understanding and support, we need all of it, I can tell you.
According to Ibinabo whose husband died of protracted illness, "my in-laws refused to allow the burial to hold until I provide a list of items and an envelope of money among them were tubers of yam, goat and others". A young widow, who in her loss of a "breadwinner" that has gulped virtually all their income in his illness to be exposed to such further expenses is an emotional trauma. To which hundreds of women in widowhood is made to experience as we caught the web of sacredness of "it's our culture".

In the case of Tosin, she said; "In all that period my life was like a horror movie with me as the lead actor. I was mostly in a trance which usually transits into a sleep that I was afraid to wake up from most times. The moment I woke up I began to pray that there should be rapture for the Lord Jesus to come and take us all home. My first two children were very withdrawn, having nightmares in their sleep, with the three year old constantly asking "mommy when is daddy coming back?" It was a question she asked for almost nine months after my husband's death. "My relationship with my in-laws immediately took a new turn; they accused me of killing my husband to inherit his property. They made all kinds of hostile moves like coming to lock up my husband's wardrobe in our bedroom. They asked for his bank account documents and other information relating to his assets. His mother went and locked up our recently completed house that we were about moving into before his death. All these happened within two weeks of his death, it was traumatizing. My husband, just 41 years was brutally murdered under such tragic circumstances and his 70 years old mother was involved in making all these devious moves with no concern of the son's children. That hit me really hard, especially with my husband being her first child, a very responsive loving son. Oh no, the man in question deserved more grieving than the scrambling for his property because all you could see is their quest to acquire his property with no pain of his tragic death. These were unfortunately some of the hard realities of his death that I would have loved for my husband to see. They cooked up all sorts of issues as they obviously were out to get at me and did not care if they were undermining the integrity of their beloved faithful son and brother even in death. With time and in this hate, my children and I drifted apart from them, and started off a new life on our own. Of course they did not bother to come looking for the children and this remained so, as I had to focus on keeping my sanity, so as to cater for my children. After his death, the estate was in a deadlock, his bank accounts were frozen and our new house locked up by my mother in-law; how did we survive I ask myself now?"

We can only ask God, He never ever fails. When a man feels that the trust of his wife is a risk and as such keeps her farther apart with his parents and siblings closest, the cost to his children is such that widows most often wish her man could be given the biblical rich man request of Lazarus but just for him to appear; it will be a great privilege for him to be seen "just once" and our question will be to ask him "if given the chance will he do it differently". "I committed myself fully to things of the spirit during this period" she continued." I learnt to trust in God and Him alone. There were times when I was down to my last dime and he showed up for me just at the nick of time". In the struggle for survival, one has to learn to first commit herself to God, he is the ultimate teammate always with the joker card of supply. God is never late, he is always on time.' Often time a widow's greatest fear is that of tomorrow, yes while living today we must plan for tomorrow but letting the anxiety of its uncertainty consume the joy of the moment is what grief is positioned to do. As a widow, one must learn to live a life of hope. Seeing the possibility of tomorrow being another day ignites a strength that hope hangs on each day.

The Shame
I feel the guilt,
had she done this
you look for fault,
I should have done that
Though many surrounds
Questions abound
As answers disappear
Never her fault to none
Assured is that
For God aware in all
Omnipresence abound

According to Tiwa "The first few years after the death of my husband were some of the most trying years of my life; I had to deal with a lot of issues ranging from accusation by my in-laws of killing my husband and the trauma they caused me on matters of his assets, my children upbringing, financial stress, loneliness, and the list was unending. My children being so young took so much emotional energy from me as they were also dealing with the loss of a loving and caring father. The weight of it all showed in every area of my life including my work, thank God for my previous good work performance of over ten years and the security of the job. The first few months of resumption at work after the funeral were not easy. My emotional instability was so severe that several of the corporate cheque I signed as signatory were returned unpaid with reason "signature irregular" as I didn't even have the presence of mind to sign my signature right. I was so troubled even when I did not realize it. In trying hard to stabilize my life, all I did was to bury myself into my work, spiritual activities and the care of my children. Thank God for my younger sister, I say a big thank you to her. She moved into my house and gave me so much company and assistance with the children that when she was leaving after two years, I wept profoundly. It seemed like losing my husband again."

The journey of a woman turns with a twist at the death of her husband. Her emotions and functions are muddled up. She's in a different "marriage", one with everything of a family excluding the husband. So the first rewarding experience of our culture is the extended family system. The strength that comes with having a sibling help hold on the kids while she learns to walk anew cannot be explained enough. It provides a temporary substitute that comes more only from her family side as her marriage family turns her a stranger and an enemy depending on the late husband's financial status.

Marriage is an emotional function built on support power; made up of husband and wife with father, mother and children building its whole. The woman is the wife and the mother with the man; the husband and father. The death of a husband cuts the wholeness of the cord thereby exposing the parts. The functional and emotional parts, which was indivisible bond in the union automatically breaks; setting apart activities that was the union. The emotional part which was the power that glue the functional parts of father, mother and children to which the woman and man performs all duties as one, now presents the parts in each one. The emotional includes the three, the love of a man, in a wife and with the family. As the woman fights with success on the kids related; the husband functions wholly exits as the wife exists. Below is my arithmetical formula that tries to explain emotional functions in our relationship to understand the loss in widowhood. At his death the woman has just two operational power to run a home that was functioning prior on four, the mother and the 'father' which is only in part; with no wife and husband even as their emotional demand still exist.

Marriage formula shows the operating the power of 4

Woman 1 (1+1) + Man 1 (1+1) ÷ 2 × 2 =4 (Mother + Wife + Husband + Father)
    Wife + Mother   Husband + Father
Whereas the widowhood formula shows the power of 2
Woman 1 (1+1) + Man 1 (1-1) ÷1 × 1 = 2 (Mother +(-Father)
    Wife + Mother   Husband – Father

Widowhood is a rough path to tread; it comes with a lot of challenges, especially the isolation. The multiplication of demand in her scarcity cannot be overlooked. As Teju said "all of a sudden I found myself feeling out of place in social circles as people looked at me either in pity or with surprise. Some of the places I loved to go to with my husband were no longer for me as people consciously or unconsciously made me feel I did not belong there anymore". One must learn to develop new interests that fit one's new profile as a widow. "I had to consciously look for responsible female singles that are able to identify with my plight to associate with, especially as pertains to loneliness, financial burden, challenges of taking on the role of the man and woman in the home". We have to learn to manage all issues, using trusted male friends and colleagues at one social and spiritual circle especially older widows or single parents who had done a good job at raising their children. "To the glory of God, I did not find it too difficult to discipline my children as I used God's Word to constantly keep them in check and on track".

It certainly helps especially as a widow when the children are introduced to God from an early age, with the parent exhibiting through words and actions, that God is the only one and the only solution. Raising children with the fear of God make the mothering job easier. As a widow, I had to moderate my lifestyle and curtail my social interactions because I did not want my children especially the female ones to see me as a liberated single mother who could do as she pleased. I made it a duty to be a role model for them by letting them know that I am a traditional and conventional woman who believes in marriage and all that it stands for and that becoming single was fate not choice. Being a widow, it pays best to double check your life in extra decency and humility for the children to imitate. It is a great sacrifice that pays the greatest. In all, as a widow there is no one formula that fixes the entire challenges one faces daily. It is only the Holy Spirit that expands perfectly in it all, as you learn each day from experience.

The shame in widowhood is clearly obvious, that is why the Lord in the Bible promised us that we will forget the reproach of widowhood. (Isa. 54:4). The beastly deed of people will multiply one shame as a widow if you don't look up to God in faith. Agnes said "I have on most occasions been faced with a situation where people come close to me and the kids pretending to be helpers when in actual sense all what they wanted was to take advantage. I recall clearly; in one of those hardest times, when I went to a friend's brother in-law who had been full of promises of help for me and the children, even with my rent. That day without food at home and no money at hand, I was stranded and didn't know what to do but to go pleading for a little assistance from him to help me feed my children. But on getting to him he boldly told me "No". He said that I either sleep with him or forget about receiving any help from him. For sure, apart from that refusal, when I did not yield to his desire; he backed out of his promise of helping me with my rent. Marvelously, that same year the Lord showed His beauty as my landlord cancelled the rent for me."

Cry if you can,
Mourn as will;
Gone forever he.
In anguish she drowns,
her soul submerged;
Darkness though abound,
Sun, moon alights
Heavy it weight
Yet Lighter the feel
As the Gilead Balm
soothes away thy feel
in a rail of reel
In time it ease,
Yet never to erase.

When Joy lost her husband, she said, "I was left alone with three kids. There was the house rent due to pay, the kids who would go to school; I had to feed and clothe them as well as cater for my own education as I was still in school then. In pain I grieved. I was confused and wondering how I will survive. People came from far and near to sympathize with me but I knew it was going to be for a while and so it was". This is so true because once the casket containing the body is lowered to the grave, with the sand offered "dust to dust, ashes to ashes", singing that song of my Anglican faith "God be with you till we meet again" as the grave is finally covered, the last "community crying" is performed. What is expected next and will be offered is refreshment no matter how little. One by one the crowd is reduced till one day you are all alone with your children. Yes, it can be that bad; not even a relation especially from the man's side will be seen, as your friends reduce. That is when and where the true crying begins. The danger of this cry is that no one will be there to comfort or console you, talk less of being there to confirm and crown your crying with a medal. This is when the crying turns to weeping. Crying can start and end as a physical exercise but weeping is sorrowful and can transcend to a spiritual and mental adventure.

Thank God for the greatest Comforter himself, to him indeed is all the glory for the souls of billions of widows who he solely consoles. This kind of weeping I tell you is about lamentation in the loneliness of a cold dark night. My sight vision worsened as a result of such, save yours if you can, especially don't cry to the gallery. There are days you would weep till daybreak or till you can never remember how and when you slept off as the sunlight alights you, are far more than the days you will peacefully go to bed asleep to wake up to the morning. Mercy said, "I have been through all kinds of challenges, emotional, financial and physical. The journey has been that of ups and downs. People's attitudes and treatment have been that of what you must have called the "beauty and the beast" with beast dominating mostly. At first, I cried, thinking about how I was going to survive, thinking that my world had ended, it was a sunset at noonday, a sudden darkness had befallen me and I did not know how I was going to survive, I could see no end to the tunnel".

So it seems to all widows at the wake of dawn until God shows the silver lining glimpsing the ray of hope to which we all follow in faith until we conquer. God in his infinite mercy has all the power to which he cuddles us. In time he begins our healing, in wiping off the tears he whispers unto one's souls his peace while blowing not just the wind of hope but lights a light of joy all around us. All must learn is to behold and embrace the situation in boldness. It is there in that thick darkness shining out to us and we must learn to look at its direction. Having to raise the kids all alone with all these trauma will not be an easy task because compared to when there were two people, all needs, wants, and desires of kids are channeled towards you, not excluding yours; but you have one who one is greater than every problem and pain. You must start by asking yourself "now that I am in charge what do I do"? Identify them, and begin in action to do them.

God Our Refuge
When a younger widow Edith told me her story, I was in shock as I thought they were stories of old tales that could not happen in this 21st century. She said, "My first journey of life as a widow began with the burial rites. I did things which were awful and looking back I can only say I allowed them because I was quite young. The whole process took about a week. All through that period; I was not allowed to lie on any bed at any point in time. I was always on the floor and I ate with a particular set of plates and cutlery which were burnt eventually. I was made to cry out around his village at 2am and then sat by his grave side between the hours of 2am to 4am after which my hair was shaved and I was taken to an evil forest where I was bathed".

In my case, I did sit on a mattress dropped on the floor when the news of my husband's death came to me as I look out to behold my state. I also drop a mattress for any woman going through the experience during that period, so that she can lie down and stretch out as she gathers her strength. Not to dehumanize her but because I say to her you need to stretch out as you are sapped of all energy. The emotional exhaustion of that news is draining and for that, stretching out with a mattress on the floor can be more soothing than sitting up in a chair, especially as you are going to be welcoming sympathizers; but it was never on a bare floor not to talk of being served as a dog. I often believe that our ancestors that started these practices and rites, their mission was never to punish the widow but was based on their understanding and belief.

But today the continual practice of those rites by us is wicked considering what we know now. In the day of ignorance grace abound, we have full knowledge of all the mythology and as such acts under wickedness. Widows are strong indeed as what they have to bear within that period is unimaginable. Even in the days of ignorance. No matter who you are, the overall experience is emotionally and physically debilitating. It is so heavy to the mind while going through so many thoughts to have to accommodate a whole lot of actions and treatments. And I get so angry when people ask, why must she condone such? Don't ask why this young lady allowed herself to be subjected to such treatment. The question should be why haven't our society outlaw such act? The time has come that such practices should be abolished. How much of these can a woman take? In her loss, her fear and her pain wrapped around her in grieving heart as she ask in shame; why me, you want her to take up another battle in a society of male dominance with her culture?

It is not her war alone because Cultural Revolution is everyone's job. Negotiation and dialogue to prevent a war is better than going to determine the winner in a battlefield because the reality is that even a winner comes out with so many lost. There still abound so many widowhood practices and rites across our Nigerian culture for women today. After twenty five years of widowhood, I find it totally unacceptable to interact and counsel widows on issues same as one experience thirty years ago. Why? Because widowhood remains the most hidden and veiled areas of violations of human rights; especially in most of our African society. The most disturbing issues of widowhood are that every rites and practices has a damaging effect and the psychological impact of it has a ripple effect on our society. There's this assumption that every dead husband is either killed or wished dead by the wife and immediately, his death opens the battle field. A woman should not be made to add another war to her battle with widowhood.

The colossal lost in her loss is more than she can comprehend. She has a fight of emotion and motion to contend with, and a woman that is battling to come to terms with the reality of her journey yet having to fight any action or deed from those around her has indeed, too much to handle. Most people would have done the same in that vulnerable state. This is love and life being torn apart. We all love to live, and the essence of life is love, family and friendship; he was the husband and the children who are the center of life are inclusive. If a woman could fight to protect her husband and his family when her husband was alive days ago, how on earth do we even imagine in our evil thought that she would turn against the family she loved so much and hate them that deep? Though that's what they are giving her, but she is too consumed by the pain and too exasperated in fear to exhume such energy. How can they not understand?

Yes they are not my blood but they are a part in my life, while we have an emotional DNA, my children are part of them; they share same DNA. We share a name and are bound in family, how is it they can't see me in my children; their nieces and nephews through their brother? It's too entangled to untangle that easily; yet, in greed they all shut their inner eyes of love. You need to have the strongest fighting spirit to be able to fight your love to break such concordant in that weak frightful state. With these emotions and in this battle a widow struggles alone as she learns to conceal her fear, pain, grief and shame in the loneliness of her path.

CHAPTER FOUR
WINNING IN WIDOWHOOD

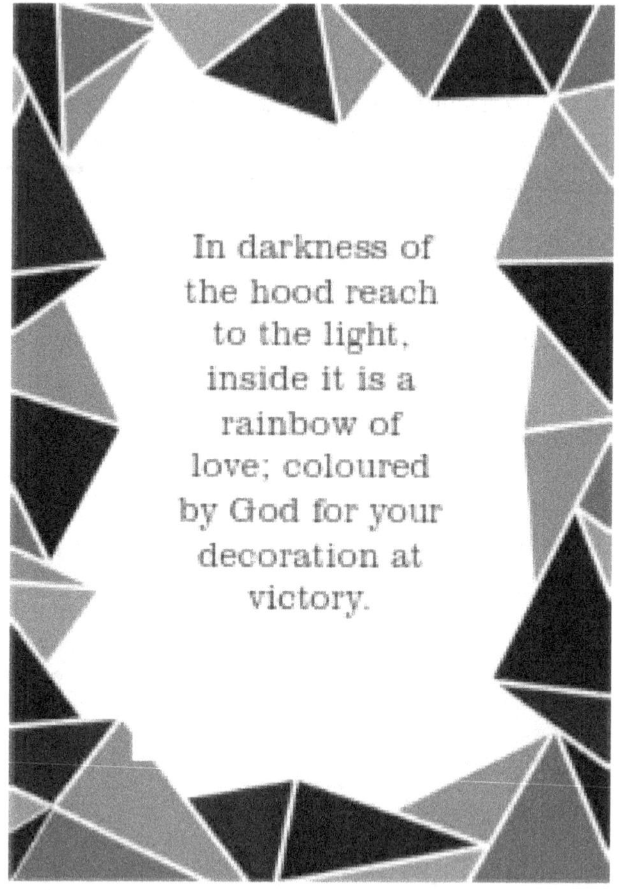

Rejoicing in hope; patient in tribulation; continuing instant in prayer;

(Romans 12:12)

Winning in widowhood is not just an individual journey. It is a collective effort of our society which must involve a conscious realization that birth and death are the two sure components of life and every other thing in between are uncertain. Even in our dexterity, it is still destiny that determines every act and actions that comes in between our life desires and plans.

It has more to do with the family knowing that she couldn't have killed or wished her husband death, and that if God has taken we can still be one family for their brother's children. Their love is part of the medication needed for the psychological wellness of their nieces and nephews which is the best they can give. Winning in widowhood for the widow is knowing also that in the walks of life, one may never do it right for all. When one sits to mourn, people will ask, are you the first woman to lose a husband. There is certainly going to be a widow around struggling hard to survive to be cited as an example of how to get up and live. But when you go to such widows, they will tell you how deaf their ears have become with names they have been called and the various abuses they have encountered while trying to work hard to provide for their homes. I remember the rumor carried about me after the death of my husband. I came back from his burial looking for extra means of income to my job so as to provide for my children.

The next story I heard was that it was being rumored that I was sleeping around with men even in my mourning dress. Surprisingly, a woman whom I thought should be more compassionate was the architect of the rumor. What some people will say to you or talk about you as well as do to you can be utterly destructive to your emotion, if you decide to take it all to heart. It is actually the insecurity of women that generates most of these theories. All you just have to understand is that God is not a man; he is a constant friend in need and will lead in his path through every tribulations. The only key is to continue to look up and trust him, keeping your path clean as can. He is the only one alive in a widow's live and in all circumstances will always bring his help and comfort. He has come with a mission of restoration of loss. Understand, the devil thought that by the death of our husbands he can destroy our lives but God is giving you abundant life in full by making it possible for us to be both father and mother.

How else could this have been possible for one person if not by double portion of His goodness? This is often what most comprehend especially his siblings as such their assumptions that one is enjoying her state of widowhood. To a widow don't let the devil take the instrument of your blessing by keeping you in fear. The magnitude of one's grief is dependent on the amount of fear exposed. And to her society, don't be deceived by the conceal of her act, behind it are pains and loneliness, the smiles and painted face is not a celebration of widowhood but deliberate decision to love life as given by the owner of life and death; which even the death in their transition must be having a share somehow where they are.

As a widow, one must learn to win by holding on to hope alone as she begin the exercise of faith thereby building resilient in the face of resistance; remembering always that nothing in life gets better without resilience. The ups and downs can be heightened or knocked down, but hope is more a choice. The chances are there to effect the change but choosing place of change can be difficult in widowhood. Yes, it can be very difficult to hold on to hope when you don't see anything positive or encouraging coming, but don't ever fail to try. It helps to nurture your faith and diminish your fear. Your gain abides in growth. The build-up of hope gradually alleviate the pain. Winning is being the father, mother and mentor; the Super 3. Another act of hope building is gratitude. You must learn to Count your blessings one by one, start by singing the song in practice. Though this may sound cliché but it will surprise you what the Lord has done in deed, if you pause to do it, you will be amazed with your testimonies despite the pain that abound. You will see the biggest blessing of the power and ability of God to you in being a husband to you, the wife, while being the father, mother and mentor to the children which is the strength of the super-widow.

Imagine that power, on your bed and in your home, within all situations and circumstances, the unseen guest is sitting in silence listening to all in our hearts cry. In his glory, he is taking you through daily by watching over you and the children, hearing both the whispers and the wishes as he ignores the murmurs in mercy; is that not awesome? For each day, you finish the day's activities and go to bed alone with no one to talk or cuddle, yet you find sleep or rest to wake to the beauty of a new day to face and overcome again alone is a conquest that is indeed awesome. A blessing worth the count cannot be more than this as it provides peace that ushers the others. As a widow, the tempest can be greater than that of an ocean but at the cliff lies countless blessings we must walk in our work every day to hold. One must learn to keep her faith with Him who lies within, overlooking the sight before her. Though many fear abound, but don't let it steal your purpose in life or kill the pleasure to live. You have a desire which is achieved in your destination not in anyone. The joy of the thanksgivings in you can outweigh the pains seen and experienced by far, especially if one we can key into it. Sing for joy even if you have to act it more than cry for pain. Believe it is all a part of the plan to the good that lies ahead.

In this tempest, what the devil does is to magnify its mission, kill, steal and destroy. He killed our husband, with the aim to steal our passion and destroy our purpose. The loss will affect our joy to live and one's hope to conquer as it inflicts pain and grief to our souls. It goes on exposing our lives in fear and shame as true happiness seems destroyed. But Christ's mission is singular in plural; that is, he has come not just to give us life back but to give it more abundantly with super ability. The abundance of life in widowhood is that ability of one person now doing what two were doing before. That is the triumphant testimony to stick to always. Rejoice in that however it is, we are stretched in abundance of moving forward the two. Forever be grateful that you are overcoming no matter the challenges, because that keeps the expectation as one abides always in hope of victory. When discouraged, burdened with loads of fears and worries, keep alive your hope simply by counting your blessings starting with that life that you have with which you are able to feel the discouragement. And one after the other, blessings line up showing how sure that abundance shines in your victories as stars in the dark night.

In break of each morn, the assurance is that as the devil is killing, God is reviving, as the devil is stealing, God is replacing; as devil is destroying, God is rebuilding. The dawn of each day shows an awesome God indeed to stand with. God has given you a voice in each stage; sing to be heard in praise, in the midst of that pain he will fulfill his purpose. Even though you feel alone, you are not alone; the Lord is with you in it all, you are his joy.

CHAPTER FIVE
SURVIVING IN THE HOOD

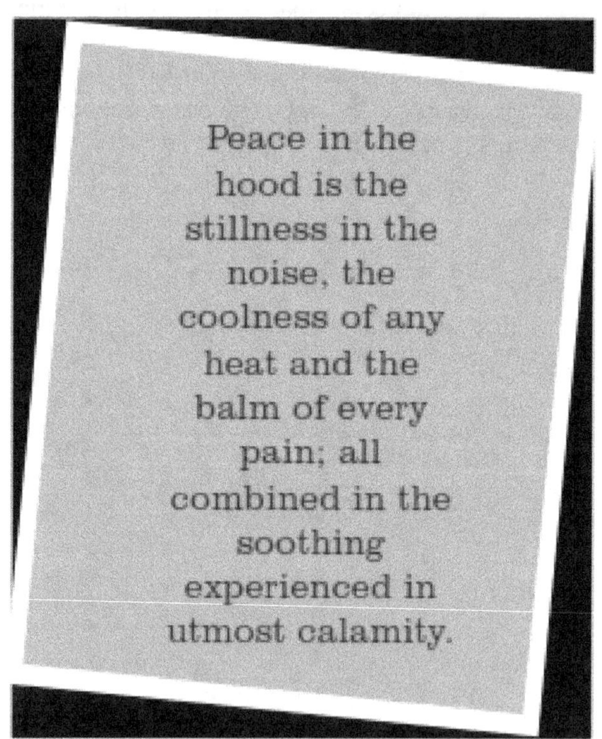

*"Peace
in the hood is the stillness in the noise, the
coolness of any heat and the balm of every pain; all
combined in the soothing experienced in utmost calamity"*

A person is made by the power of his or her thoughts and as a widow with all emotional strength gone; you can be torn apart by self-condemnation and that of the people if not careful. The unanswered questions of it: if, why, how and what, especially "why me", can make you believe it must be as a result of your sins or shortcomings in prayer. The Word of God that says, "All have sinned and come short of the glory of God" (Rom 3: 23) can stop being true to you as a widow if care is not taken.

The culture and society in their behaviour will further drown one in condemnation starting with the rites. Most often the treatment to widows are more in acts that violates a woman's dignity; making one feel ashamed. If widowhood is as a result of sin, there will only be widows and widowers with no married woman or man otherwise this God's word cannot be true. You can be led by the society as the devil to believe that you caused your sorrow by highlighting all your shortcomings with our culture affirming to the belief with what you have to undertake. But we thank God for his Word to which religion, especially Christianity must balance out. To survive you must being again. Take a self-ride to your teenage girl and find that girl and bring her to the woman standing alone and begin to work to key her into the woman in between the both. Bring the three personalities together with the power to do great things desired in unison. Having first build your faith using God's promises as we agreed to affirm that it is not your sin but the will of God. You must able to manage your thoughts well as all the humiliating practices and expectations of people.

We must also begin to call on our society to address, and be that as it may, abolish all cultural practices and rites that heighten the shame and pain of widowhood. In times past before Christianity took deep root, a widow in my culture had to dress in complete black for months but that has changed, reducing the official months for the ceremonial mourning. The shame of the dressing ranges from identification to segregation because with such dressing you are recognized anywhere you enter. Imagine dressing in black mourning clothing for two years as before. It must be psychologically destructive as it will keep you in a depressed state throughout, knowing that you are limited in words and actions as well as acceptance. When a friend of mine lost her husband I personally told her that she should block her ears to overcome, because of what she will hear. Whether you sit in solitude or move around, people will have something to say. So you should decide which is better, do you sit down and beg for alms that you may never get or you get with insults or to go out and fend for your home as capable and with dignity?

To walk through the life struggle and experience as a widow, one must learn to win her five senses. The psychological wellness of a widow helps immensely in her survival and to get that you must master the act of understanding and forgiveness. The physical provision of a widow is God's abundance which she must stretch to collect. The Lord said that there is no food for the lazy man (Pro. 12:27) and that he will bless the work of our hands (Deut. 28:12). We must seek and ask him to give one a fertile ground to cultivate as we watch him grow it for our use mightily using all that is within us to begin. In your effort to provide as the man and woman of your home, you will encounter all forms of abuses; while the men shower you with physical abuse, the women will dry you up with their tongue towel of gossip especially when God's goodness is obvious around you. Hard work will certainly be overlooked as most is quick to credit it to promiscuity. The social, physical, emotional and spiritual survival in widowhood is a collective package: you are widowed, wounded and desperately in need of skills and abilities to continue to conquer every obstacle in it all.

Planning for the future in his loss can be a big issue. One can lose the sense of motivation and the desire to plan or dream big again. Some often develop an underlying feeling of inadequacy or incapability, especially for a woman who once had a man leading the way and charting the course for the family but now finds herself taking on this role of leading and taking the initiative for the future. It can be a very scary situation. When a woman loses her spouse, there are so many uncertainties that present themselves; this can affect the woman in her actions. Questions will stamped your mind. Will or do I remarry? What will be the implications if I remarry? Will I need to relocate? When and where? Can I go through this alone? How can I accomplish life alone? How do I dream and what's going to happen to the woman in me? These and more countless questions with no answers as well as people's own questions, attitude and treatment can truly be overwhelming. In a society like my where counseling is not a common practice with the best coming from Pastors; yes God has all the answers and solutions to it all but it is often not as easy as we think when we use Christianity which deals with spirituality alone, forgetting the relevant of application of real life encounters.

Her physical and mental health is so under nourished especially in society that it has been confirmed that widows are largely omitted. Taking charge of one's life is a vision that must be seen in his death as you move on from denial to acceptance of the situation. To grow with a mission to conquer the race you must leave the 'how' and 'what' to 'when' by focusing on the 'now'. Life itself is filled with so many uncertainties but the life of a widow though so bleak can only be certain with God. Just personify Him all round you as you get up, get out and get going. I have heard about lemon and lemonade. The popular quote, "when life gives you lemons make lemonade" It's very true. However, in the life evolution of widowhood I have learnt that the first thing to do is to find value in the situation. It is very difficult but once done, the pains become less, peripheral and purposeful. I say, when life gives you lemon, find the value in its taste. Lemonade can be tasteful but it is a mere substitute and a secondary effect for lemon which is the primary factor that remains underneath will spring up the acrid taste.

To continue to add the ingredients to neutralize the lemon of widowhood which is what the everyday life experiences will be doing, can be time consuming, energy sapping and treasure draining. That will be a distraction, a delay and a distortion most often. If I continue to add sugar to the lemon, one can run out of supply even on a temporary basis and the effect can be a great hindrance or delay to your journey but learning to find value in its sour taste is letting those experiences not deter your drive as you move to conquer. Seeing the sour taste of the lemon as a part of the flavor gives it a value. Finding examples is in the sufferings of Christ, Jesus saw the value in his death and took the lemon. (Heb 2:9-18). I often wonder if Nelson Mandela made lemonade by taking the various opportunities presented, will his story, the apartheid and South Africa be the same as today. Everything works together for good to them that love God. (Rom 8:28) means that the taste of lemon though sour yet taste good in a different way as its path of the bricks that will work together for one's good. Widowhood sucks is a common phrase but widows rocks is another; meaning life is still good even in her loss. My best phrase to new grieving widow is that life will get better in an entirely different way; meaning while the sour taste of widowhood remains the sweet savor taste of life is in it still.

We must understand that we are a three part being; spirit, soul and body. This is crucial, for in that one can move the three self-parts. As the people in Gen 11: 2 who came to a plain land and agreed together to build a tower, we must work together in unison oneself with even in that pain to taste the lemon of life in His death. You learn to enjoy life by ignoring every bitter experience it presents to you with acceptance, understanding and completely with more attention to the Strength, Weakness, Opportunity and Threat of every day journey. Through that you move each day taking steps and authority, saying now that I'm in charge what do I do in all that you encounter?

ACTION ONE
In this journey, the protection of our children and home must be utmost practice. Whoever our friend male or female must be, they have to be one that value God, family and the moral ethics of life. How your friends are must be of great

importance as they will affect your lifestyle and that of your children. There's need to expand your business or add one to your work if you are working, as time permits never neglecting your motherhood, and watch God settle you in joy overtime.

The children remain the greatest source of strength and happiness today and tomorrow. Failing as a mother to me is worse than failing as a wife, though both are the true parameters of success for a virtuous woman. But if one can be said or assumed to have killed the husbands, widows, fight in war room of prayer and boardroom of survival to shut their mouths and confuse their thoughts by raising the children right. The beauty of this success is that we will be called blessed by the same people and more. Make your mothering responsibility a 'major' always. It is a major in our course of life more so as a widow because God will improve one little effort in the 'elective' as a father. Introduce new business ideas that can complement your work or existing one. I always suggest adding a daily income business. Being the man and the woman now, and taking up all responsibilities, things must change. The first thing to do is to pause all expenses except the basics that have to do with feeding, fees and health care while saving up and planning hard for the rent and investment as the case will be. In as much as I disagree with sympathizers deciding the lifestyle and budget expenditure for a widow, as it often increases her shame; it is a necessary look into by her.

A good friend should learn to support her psychologically without a pity attitude. As a friend or relative you do not just go to tell her how to and what not to do especially when she comes to you as a friend for financial assistance. For her to swallow the pride in her to face the shame of coming to ask means it is a necessity to her. It will be more helpful to find whatever you can and give no matter how little, in a much later date present to her your advice. Her emotion is a land mine, after all imagine a human being torn constantly between pain and grieve while battling with fear and shame muddled in her lone path, as she faces more suspicions around, making an irrational decision and actions are bound to be more likely than not, if not for the overwhelming grace of God. Showing a good level of understanding in compassion is a gift widows seek in their friends as they journey through recovery. Don't be discouraged by the difficult, lazy and entitled ones, as a friend, brother or sister you have an obligation to help her navigate. So you must discharge it humbly and firm, because if you don't and play the apathy the sin will be yours but once said and not received it becomes hers. Always show empathy in your sympathy to her for in so doing will you remain objective and loving.

A HELPFUL TIP

From experience and that of other victorious widows I have met, it is best to pause on clothes shopping. After all you were not naked before his death and as well the first few years of his death is associated with grief so what's the celebration for clothing and fashion. Being trendy in fashion is not bad but getting into it can add undue pressure, it is better to buy beautiful sturdy things than the vague in vogue ones. Shopping for the children is very important especially in festive seasons so that their sadness does not increase with the emotion of if daddy were here; this can cause some psychological problems on them. We must learn to manage most things they have well as it will certainly reduce the burden. Any inability to cater for our children's needs can result in them having a complex which affects their self- esteem. Some children have been known to cultivate bad friends and character in the lack. You should understand very well that one can never heal the pain in their hearts with frivolous buying rather one can spoil them. Their emotional loss cannot be replaced by any material things. What they need most is you and your love. Create time and things you do with them, play, share stories even fictions.

Do more of the fun things children love to do with them especially with young kids. Be sure to be more than you use to be while you do more than you used to do without burning the both end of your candle. This helps create greater bond while providing the security and assurance they desire. The children needs an affirmative display of home that showcases life is still good even without a father, this is what their hearts are longing most in their loss. Most importantly keep them close to God's word and works, pray and teach them to love God; it is only in Him with your love and attention will they find healing in time for life to blossom again. The journey of survival I assure you is enormous, even if you think that you have enough, with the husband's death. No matter the cash at your disposal at the time of his death, it is never enough if not well managed, because the task ahead is unpredictable and almost unending in a lone lane; especially when you have young children. When I see young widows living extravagantly, I feel very uncomfortable. It is expedient that we appreciate the fact that in his prudence and seeming denial, he saved up what he left. His spirit must have seen today in his yesterday, don't take it for granted. Don't see him as a miser but "wiser". Use every dime rightly in reverence to his wisdom. Let's respect the fact that If he had spent it as we might have desired and expected, one wouldn't have been left with much at his demise. The journey is not just far but the road to the destination is very rocky, as such you are going to fall often especially at the beginning.

Lola said, "I am looking for money now to set up my business; I can't seem to forgive myself. To think of the $700 I had that was more than enough to set it up, that I wasted, makes me want to hit my head on the wall". This is a very common and an understandable experience. While you learn the steps of this new path in time, be wise and take every step light and rightly. The busyness of this road at the beginning should not deceive one in knowing that this is a lone path which requires a great deal of work and walk. There is no possibility of estimating the cost at its end, talk less at its beginning. So keep your pace slow in all things so when you fall it won't lead to a crash. Remember there are no king horses and men of your own that will come running to put you together. One must try at all times to run in such a way that if one falls, it will be a bruise, so as to be able to get back up on one's own. All the sympathizers and their supports that are coming if you are lucky, do not last for long as the traffic on the road you are seeing disappears before you with the slap of the sour taste of the lemon landing hard on your cheek as it defines the reality, leaving you too lonely yet busier than before.

Take a firm grip of every savings and assets. Hold on tight, guarding jealously every dime. It will never be "go ask your daddy" nor will it be, "this is what I have to support please let's do it" or whatever means you both were using together. The formula of two-become-one in marriage arithmetic has changed to one equals to two raised to power two; whatever the math you come up, the solution is all your own alone. Everyday presentation screams to your glare "now that I am in charge", an authority that can be misused, if not careful. Always seek for God wisdom and guidance in everyday dealing. His wisdom he gives freely if asked (Pro 2:6), this help us build better knowledge and understanding of the journey. Without him you will not only fall but you will fail in strength to rise. The hand of man will fail you especially that one you are leaning on when least expected. But God's guidance is a sure and best direction to follow for he alone directs every arm of flesh that will help.

Planning how to spend the money inherited, earned or given after his death should not be immediate. It's best to keep all money away as much as possible; spend on basics. Give yourself time to heal emotionally, yes the scar will remain forever but the pain will reduce in time. In order to heal fast you must streamline your friends and activities by readjusting realistically in all, especially as you try to understand the journey. Those friends that you use to go on shopping and spending spree with when your husband was alive tactfully withdraw, though one expects such friends to be helpful and supportive by not inviting or explaining the entire shopping expenditure to you anymore. People may ask, how do you select your friends? One of the sure ways of knowing who to cut off as a friend in widowhood is determined by how helpful they are to you in adjusting to your new found status. Such friends, who will not only tell you the stories of their husbands' allowances, gifts and loving but are inviting you to these shopping, please do away with them without hesitation. Even if she wants to buy for you, it is not uplifting in anyway; it adds more pain to already saddened heart. In helping a widowed friend, it is better to give her the money and she will use it for her most pressing needs. Remember she is going to be responsible for the capital and recurrent expenses of the home; it is no longer the husband will pay the rent and fees while you manage the allowance given to you on the home needs with your own income. You are going to do it all, you are absolutely in charge. I tell widows, as a 'father' of your children now; you can build houses for the children to inherit.

Think from this angle, to educate and train my children is one of the many assets; don't be satisfied with just that; you can build empire for your kids. It is the power of the mind. As a widow, thinketh, so is she. (Pro 23: 7). James Allen in his "As a Man Thinketh" said "a person is limited only by the thought he chooses". You are now a two whole number raised to two in one and can achieve the purpose of the two. If you process your thought to that; your actions will be directed to it.

REJECT THE ENTITLEMENT MENTALITY

"Seek thou your support" when I suggest this in a "widow's creed", I do not mean it from the angle of alms. One being widowed should not place self to be a beggar. Being a widow is not a charitable establishment; her support should be more creative rather than provision opportunities. As much as we solicit their understanding, one should not feel entitled to it. Expectation of understanding should not debar us from standing for ourselves, you will best be understood when one only stoop to conquer. This helps one in standing to install. Looking for who will help you and being angry when not assisted and holding a grudge is an entitlement mentality. To get an understanding from anyone; family, friends or foe is a privilege not a right; after all we are talking of them being conscious of our plight or state. Remember that some cannot easily deduce the difference. We must always understand this fact. I have seen widows grumbling on who has and hasn't helped while narrating the rights to which they deserve to such help.

One should not hinder her blessings with grudges; it produces anger and bitterness which certainly overloads the body and emotion with unhealthy rubbish. The empowerment to stand is solely one's responsibility and no one else fault when you fall; your desire will certainly motivate your actions. What is your desire; to be placed on grants and aids or to be an aid? My deduction from widows I have met is that what they desire directs all they do. If one desire is channeled on expectation that people are supposed to sympathize and help, one will become less productive driven and more dependent oriented.

Learn to channel your energy to your work and if angry face your God and your work. With such an attitude, though you may never get it all completely right; it keeps you on the right track at all times. This is the motion to keep, as it builds your self-esteem making you an authority in all authority. It is very important as a widow to pray always to God to provide someone that will bless you, while praying to be a blessing to someone as well. Despite the circumstances you are in, look out for a way to add value you have found in the lemon taste to your life. Put something positive in the lives of others for in so doing, you find pleasure that surpasses your pain.

PLANNING TO WIN

As you are cutting your expenses add up to your income generating avenue. You can go from petty selling to big businesses as your status permits. Adding that to your office work is very important especially at an early stage where you have young dependent children. The idea should be anything that can give you daily or weekly income. Most women do have problems of financial management, the spontaneous buying of all sorts especially in beauty and fashion stuff are issues we all must learn to conquer. Imagine a wife where the husband had been providing virtually all things including housekeeping allowance, her salary or business proceeds are used to augment at her discretion. Being not only denied of such luxury but has to manage whatever income she gets on such home, is going to be tough. She will require some time to learn. Adjusting to such situation is going to require a lot of emotional management and self-discipline. It entails a great deal of learning and it is in a special school with no curriculum or syllabus; yet has difficult courses. With no assigned teachers and theories propounded varying.

The only teacher you will have is God's guidance and mentoring. The experiences are the course contents and learning process is based on the trials while the error forms the next course content. It takes time and there is no graduation period as the course advances itself overtime. There can be a danger of great damage when one fails, especially at the beginning, for weight every experience critically. In this school, some women have not only been confused but have been reduced from their would-have been buoyant financial status to absolute poverty. I do always share my sympathy with such women, for I tell you, it is not easy at all. I know a rich widow whose husband's big business disappeared shortly after his death. Her issue was complicated because not only did she have to learn this new life management course, but she had to learn to work as she was a beauty and a mother care product at home when the husband was alive. In her case, while learning this new course, she also had to learn what and where her husband's businesses were. Her course program was too large for her comprehension as her cognitive domain had been weakened her emotion and psychomotor rendered effectively inactive. As such most people swindled her out of the resources she would have used for the children's upkeep with ease before she knew what was happening. What I say to widows based on experiences is that they should not go into huge investment immediately, take it little by little as you learn and grow, especially if you were not in business before. A widow's husband's entitlement was swindled off her in the name of business. She, as a teacher had never done any form of trading before only to be deceived by crooks with mouth-watering importation deal.

She actually invested all her inherited money and lost big time. But for God, his mercies and her job, she would have gone back to the village to face the scavengers of her in-laws. If you want to invest go into land and property, if you have substantial capital making sure you use reputable company. A good land no matter the remoteness will grow your money later while keeping it safe. There are other investments, you can read up and seek expert advice especially when you have the capital and not into business before. Be wary of friends and relatives, there are definitely good ones but to minimize your in-house enemy use professional advice and services. A genuine relative or friend can suggest something that accidentally doesn't go too well as expected; and this is bound to affect your relationship and with already reduced number we have; it is better to keep the few around. A widow at an early stage of bereavement is vulnerable, no matter how strong a personality one has, you are emotionally deprived and psychologically drained as such often most things decided or done in such state produces poor result.

All you need from day one is your basic provision of shelter, feeding, schooling and healthcare. Concentrate on any business no matter how small that can provide daily income first while your emotion stabilizes. For all it's worth, women should not agree to be housewives, though it is no longer fashionable for women to be full time housewives. The concept of men seeing her as part of his property in the house has produced theories of woes for so many widows and their children as siblings and managers struggle and collect as many as they could grab. The men should learn not only to involve their wives in all your businesses and investments but get her to work. She needs all knowledge and information as the power of attorney to take up the responsibility of raising the children as she manages the greedy and wicked relations and colleagues in case the unexpected happens. A wife remains a man's true partner with one shared capital, the children, as well as the husband of the woman. Ngozi, a widow is still having a paper of her husband's land, the exact location of which she doesn't know because he never took her there. The supposed lawyer of the late husband eventually sold the land. The heart of man is desperately wicked (Jeremiah 17: 9). She said when she confronted the lawyer he threatened her life. Yes, she let it go, the fear in her is enough, and one does not need more. They energy and money of going to court with lawyer on land she knows no exact God will certainly judge such a man; her nights of weeping in agony and despair will never be in vain, but the system must begin to protect the widow starting with the husband.

I encourage women, to help protect their sisters in widowhood. The wives of these callous men, get your husband to and please pray for them husbands as you remain very watchful, for any widow friend or relative; ensure that she is not victimized by him for the sake of our children. We as a sheep can be helpless but together we can be helpful. Widowhood is in the life evolution of every married woman and the protection of a widow is the protection of a next generation. Like Pilate, wash off your hands and those of your children in matters of humiliating a widow where you can't help, using at least your voice to state you're not a participant of every ill. A widow's cry at midnight is one no one wants to bear because even God detest to hear the cry of a widow. Be assured, it is a rocket of painful emotion fired to God and the effect of such is the wrath of God which we may never know where, how and when it will descend. In widowhood, one's greatest fear is survival which we strive to conquer. It is very possible even in all impossibilities because our God who is greater than all impossibilities. (Matthew 19: 26).

When my husband died I had my teaching job with a mini shop, and I also added procurement business. While my convenience shop was making sure that I took care of our daily needs, the bread and butter table demand; my salary was there for the school fees and the procurement dividend I used for rents and investment whenever it comes. I believe in land investment, if you see a genuine one buy it even in remotest area, it will always grow and which you can resell. I benefited from it. One biggest problem I had to learn to conquer is developing financial discipline; yes, having the 'his' attitude to 'hers' will not be easy for most of us. Naturally, unlike men, most women are clothes shoppers. A woman's wardrobe can be 80-90% filled, not bad because we must look good, but our men with the 10-20% never looked bad either. With that small wardrobe he dressed himself handsomely for all occasions. I had to learn this equation as widow in adopting the man's attitude. I learnt not to buy everything admired or that is in vogue to consistently look good.

You do not need to reduce drastically the dress sense but you can shop wisely, packaging your wardrobe in a way that it does not take up your budget and plunge you into debt or depression. Some widows are constantly in debt because they couldn't manage their finances well, leading them to so many embarrassing situations and some social stigmatization. The best policy to managing our personality in this circumstance as I have discovered is to find your inward beauty and personality. Finding you and reshuffling your wardrobe effectively through reorganization will help you look best always without looking or feeling the same most times. With this, you will develop a carriage and style that helps you in dressing right without buying always. The emotional torture of not looking your best can make one lose self-confidence or drag one to lack of self-control, but getting the best from our inward satisfaction is what we need most. We all as individuals have a "that" that others admire outwardly and inwardly, I call it "God given selling point on you". Find yours if you haven't done so, ask God and he will help you to build your confidence and esteem as you stand tall even in your petite to shine wishing that your "that". It's your innate beauty.

With a beauty within every other looks are secondary. I have learnt to remind myself that I am wonderfully and fearfully made in the image of God's beauty (Psalm 139: 14). I look into the mirror and I see beauty that I do not deserve, so when occasion that demands the buying of social uniform (Asoebi) or new cloth comes up, I can decide depending on the situation either to buy; go without it or not go at all without feeling sad. By experience, this is one of the conditions in widowhood if not properly managed, has emotional implications of sadness that can increase your grieves because it makes you lament. If you don't get your peace in an esteemed position, then life makes you mourn perpetually as you continue to complain and grumble. This can create some feelings of anger, bitterness and resentfulness especially to those who had their husbands providing virtually everything for them. It can even expose one to abuse of self and children. As a widow if you fail to find your peace with a self-esteem and empowerment, you can subconsciously develop an underlying jealousy, anger and bitterness towards the married friends and acquaintances which sometimes leads to withdrawal. This can be dangerous to one's own welfare physically and spiritually.

OUR GREATEST WORK OF ALL

Training the children should be the major concern of any woman especially once widowed. All finances should be wisely invested on their education and welfare, because once they have good upbringing, a good education and the right exposure; with a good job, career or skill, their story will change to glory overcoming all the gory and so will your name. When the husband was there, no matter how little his provision, it was a sure relief but taking up the entire responsibility is a big one that demands total adjustment in lifestyle. Widowhood is the most difficult state of the entire Hood. It does not resemble the childhood, although being a girl child is tough. While being a woman is tougher, it is totally different from that of wifehood and motherhood. In childhood people are responsible for your life, mostly parents and guardians. As for wifehood, your husband is supposed to be for you and the children, while you as a mother; you have a supportive role in the home irrespective of the unseen reality at times. A man is the head as it is said in the Holy Book, whereas, the woman is the help mate. A wife's position from creation was that of support. The man seen as the firm with her woman the frail, though not the servant as they both wheel the boat of their house. That is why when you move from father's hand to husband's the transformation is mutual. In motherhood, being your mother's daughter makes the transitory experience easier to absorb as children appear but being a widow is the toughest; nothing actually prepares you for it. One learns to be a husband to self, while remaining the mother; you are actually three in one in emotion and "two raised to power two" in actions and not two as mostly assumed by many people.

One must learn to work as the husband, the wife and the mother while managing the emotions as wife, husband, mother and care-giver. The needs and duties of these will continue to arise for her to fill or manage. They are indeed task up beyond the hill that one learns to climb in the journey of widowhood. In a culture and society with no functional policies and facilities, the steep is unimaginable as obstacles are massive. Remember as a wife, I was mostly seen or being the neck supporting the head. How easy do you think it will be for this neck to form back a head when cut off without your support? Practically impossible, but we have to devise a way to live not just to exist. In all this is what we have to contain in life at the hood. Thank God for the grace he gives, that's truly each widow's uses to succeed in this project of our life. I call it a project because you will be exposed to variables which will certainly influence your total being; motions and emotions. But in all things, don't give up. God will never abandon you (Hebrew 13:5). He is the one variable that is constant in his actions. He moves people to help only, so rely not on them because they can refuse to be used by not moving. When the person you depend as your propeller refuses to move, you will be stock; thereby resulting in your fall or stagnating in their bondage. It's best to look up to God as you work to earn your respect knowing that every help comes from him. (Psalm 121).

The Shortness of a Man's Arm

The alms of man are as short as their arms. As a widow, don't place your hope on people. They are bound to disappoint and when they do; the effect can be destabilizing. But when you put it in God and a person fails, you immediately look beyond the disappointment with faith and in your belief you will see the real appointment that God has for you. He's the only faithful one (Hebrew 10: 23). He is an anchor that is very supportive at all times; and in all circumstances. In my early days in the Hood, one of those days my children had to go back to school and I needed financial assistance, I approached a relative who promised to help. I had my hope on his promise and so made no other effort both in prayer and practice. All my efforts to get him to fulfill the promise at the proposed time failed. The pain and confusion of that day made me thereafter never to hope on anyone. Rather, I expect from people while praying to God to do it. It is certain that it is through people that God blesses but trusting in God is one's ability to place hope in him not in any human being. It is a lesson I learnt that day, as God taught me that all help comes from Him by giving me the money I needed from where I never expected. It is not him or her that is doing it, while appreciation and gratitude are key, understanding it is God doing it through them helps one build respect to man and reverence to God. We will forever be grateful to those helpers, for allowing God to use them to compliment in all seasons. Our prayer is that God's fountain of goodness surrounds them all around you as they continue to do their good deed.

Our Joy in the Hood

In the process of the journey, I had a great conviction that in all needs and with prayers, God will use even the devil to provide my needs. In that, I learnt to seek in dignity as I accept in humility whatever I get in as I strive to survive. To be physically engaged, I have learnt with time has helped in keeping me away from abuse and temptation. As it's said that an idle mind is indeed the devil's workshop, when you don't occupy your mind with work; the loneliness can be more and will expose one to all forms of abuses. This will not only diminish yourself worth in public but make you ashamed even in your privacy. A widow needs all the encouragement she can get from relatives, friends, church and even colleagues in words and deeds but without herself in the equation; she won't be encouraged. The financial and moral support is very good but without a social support, finding herself back becomes cumbersome. The joy of the widow is often misinterpreted by most as her joy in his death. While the widow in her fear of being seen to be celebrating his death drowns herself in misery as the society in their own fear avoids her in social inclusion. We must learn to loosen our uptight position with death, knowing it is a circle of life controlled by the owner. Remember, every ill word receives destroy a soul as the good ones build it, so also is every good or bad act, but the degree of these actions are magnified in widowhood because of her loss especially because of our stigma .

The treasure box of widowhood is filled with pain, making every act of kindness the greatest with the givers most cherished. They come in words and deeds. The notion that what a widow need most is financial assistance is a fallacy. The physical, emotional and spiritual well-being is an embodiment of every human desire and a great asset in building one's finances. The beauty of that hymnal 467 "life is great, so sing about it"
"Life is great! Whatever happens?

Rainfall or sunshine, joy or pain,
Hardship, grief or disillusion,
Suffering that I can't explain
Life is great if someone loves me,
Holds my hand and calls my name"

There are people that I hold dearly to my heart, you cannot imagine what those words like "my dear you are trying, you are strong, you are blessed, thank God for your life, what two people are doing with great difficulty you are doing alone and not doing badly for yourself" etc. Those words are literally the same as the last two sentences of the song. It is as fulfilling as the material gifts I have received from others. As much as we are doing even more than our state, there is this fear of not doing enough, but with such words of appraisal comes greater motivation. It's like hearing your spouse say "I love you". It is a rewarding feeling. In supporting a widow around you, at all times with or without material gifts, have something motivating in words to say. Such, I tell you, is highly uplifting in spirit to her. A good word they say is good to the soul (Proverbs 16: 24) especially to disheartened soul of a lonely widow. When you feed her with good words it makes it easier to adore and reverend your critic. I have a brother in my church that I look forward to seeing because he always has a good word that is capable of diffusing the worst of my emotions.

To all those who have spoken comforting words to me and all my sister widows, I say a big "thank you" and may God count it for you in heaven as your labor of love. These words, I tell make the hearts lighter while soothing her soul; it strengthens the zeal in her even in the most trying times. Do you know the best nights are those nights we go to bed with echoes of such words ministering to our hearts? It stocks up joy in the spirit that puts a smile on our face that no matter the condition we are able to heave a sigh of relief in the comfort of our lone bed. Such words assure her that she is not only doing well, but that people are seeing her effort. As a widow, we have taken up employment that is predominantly a man's job, taking up such a job entails an extra effort to which we are daily struggling with and being complimented often eases the tension. That's what those good words do to a weak widow; it's a soul booster. It helps in diffusing the fear while building her strength. It actually reduces the pains and helps in taking the reproach of our widowhood away (Isa. 54:4). When you establish this compassionate heart with her, whatever you see which is not right in her; with that same kind affection you will tell her and she'll will take with great interest. In all, in your words we see can see hopelessness and pain or hope in helplessness, support in our segregation and reassurance in difficult situations that helps in drying our tears mostly in the loneliness of the night as it fills our heart with a definition of success.

God Our Shield

Since the death of my husband, one thing that has sharpened my perception of life and the power of God in his words was the attitude of people around namely family, friends and colleagues. I happened to be a police widow and the story of their widows remains a pathetic tale for another day. After my husband's death at the apex of my grieving were afflictions, first was ejection from the quarters. Six weeks after his death, as I came back from the village, I had three different officers coming to show me their allocation letters to the house I was occupying. One of them I remember got the house allocated to him before his burial as the date of the letter was about eight days after his death, I remember asking, "Sir, you could not even wait for him to be buried before taking up his house". Finally, the fight reduced to one officer. This man and the system were a terror to my life as letter of ejection was pasted on the front door of my house with his entitlement yet to be paid.

Being a staff in the establishment did not help in their consideration either. The pain of their treacherous attitude sent me to sleep every night I am lucky to get sleep, wakes me up every morning and walk around with me all day. In my trauma and the instability of my thought, it took me a long time before I could recognize the man that was to move into my house; as he weekly stopped me to remind of the need for me to move out so that he can pack into his house despite the fact that he was living in a house. Our first introduction and last contact remains vivid in my memory. He introduced himself the first time, telling me how nice a man my husband was, that if not for him when he newly came on transfer, lots of officers humiliated him and using tribal forces to frustrate him as they made the place a hell for him. My husband he said singlehandedly fought for him and that he was a very nice man. He truly sang praises of all his kindness and love. This is a story I heard only from him never from my husband, his testimony though did not deter him from adding more grief to my already aggrieved situation. Immediately after his praises he told me that he has "won the battle" for the allocation of my house. This is barely two months after my husband's death. It is in writing this book that it occurred to me that he must have purposely planted himself at least once every other week on my path way to work, to ask me when I was packing out and I will answer "as soon as I am paid his entitlement so I can get money to rent a house," as politely as I could.

Our last encounter was, as usual when he accosted me, he said that he wanted to get married and he didn't want his wife to stay at his current apartment where they shared common facilities, as I quote him "I don't want my wife to share bathrooms and toilets with barracks women". He suggested that I should move into his apartment with my children so that he can move into the house. I looked at him in anger, with pain I asked "if not for my husband's death, will you dare stand and say this to me, my husband being your senior makes me one too and besides I was once living in such apartment before moving to this present one". In pain, crying I warned him sternly never to stop me again on this way or anywhere for that matter, otherwise he should lend me the money to rent a house and I will move out the next day and pay him once I get the entitlement. To the glory of God he never stopped me again and three months later, apart from being paid my entitlements. Finally, my late brother-in-law paid for a house and I moved out with my children after some months. I never saw the man until months after, as we drove into the quarter for an official commitment, my attention was drawn by my driver to some people that were talking and pointing at me. I ignored him and them facing my business after all they are on their own so I was not bothered. I have more issues in life than that, I said.

As we drove out, a former neighbor frantically waved me down and running unto me said "Madam, have you heard?" "What?" I said, calling his name she said he is dead, as I shouted what and how; she told me a bizarre story that till today remains a mystery. This man as I later learnt moved into the house in January because I moved out by November of the previous year; and on one faithful day in March, exactly the same date my husband embarked on that journey of no return he was shot dead. After our last encounter I never saw, heard or even remember thinking of him. I did go later to condole with the yet to wed wife, whom I saw for the first and last time that day. After his service of song in Lagos, as his body was being taken home, so also were all his property including his yet to wed wife living the house empty. A house he spent one year, eight months struggling with a widow whom he professed of the husband's goodness and two months renovating, he lived in it barely two months. It showed the desperate wicked heart of man (Jeremiah 17: 9) how the mind of God is completely different from man's (Isaiah 55:8).

As I was battling with the accommodation problem, barely four months after my husband's death, I got to work one day, as I walked into the entrance, I saw some colleagues that gathered by the notice board, looking towards me as I approached the notice board. My very good friend, God blesses her soul walked up to me trying to stop me from entering. I, curiously in a worrisome mood, forced myself through her to see what was happening. Right on the Notice Board was my suspension letter pasted for all to see. My offence I did not know as I have neither a copy of the suspension letter nor copies of warnings or queries on any account of gross irresponsibility, insubordination or indiscipline that resulted to the suspension without pay. Under four months of life, I went from being a wife to being widowed, jobless and homeless. I lost all but my four kids, who helped me to hold "me" as I almost lost myself in my loss. No husband, no source of income, how did I cope? I ask myself today as I write. God is faithful. I remember seeing it and with tears I turned back saying to myself and friend "thank God let me even go and face my accommodation problem" because the police were threatening to throw us out and if they can do this to me at work, they will certainly throw my children and I out like a piece of garbage on the street, for sure.

You may ask, aren't they aware you lost your husband? And I say to you, they buried my husband in a ceremonial way barely four months ago. They have not given me any cash support not as individual or organization, talk less of his entitlement. I as well works in the same establishment, how else can I make them know, if they are "unknown" with all these? Nothing will bring them to know as it happened to be a fact later. That day, I had to leave the school to face my accommodation problem. I remember going to plead for the reversion of my suspension, but it fell on a dead conscience. Do you know my offence as I later realized? My window has been broken and all are looking in. My covering has been pulled off as I appeared naked to all. Seeing what is desired, in want they reach for it. When it could not be taken easily, they work to take it by force; by breaking the tiny 'will of strength' believed left for me by inflicting more pain on me. All glory to God for that "something inside so strong", it is amazing how God uses that himself perfectly to strengthen one in this journey. The abuse and exploitation that one goes through in widowhood cannot be told completely. It is most terrible in our Nigerian society, when out of fear and shame you cannot talk and even in bravery you talk, will you be heard or believed? I remember the last time after I had settled my accommodation; I went to plead for my job and got the same response.

In most encounters one is made always to understand she has what I called "play to win a widow's woe game". You find we have a card each with a table. Like I was told, all I need to do is to play mine to get his. As I left with my same 'No queen' card, stating affirmatively that I will come back at God's own time; he kept his ' No king '. I truly didn't know how I was able to hold on to my sanity then; as painful and grieving as I felt, my faith was resolute with no tears to shed that day. And to God be the glory he heard my voice because in less than two months, there was a change that the beast out and brought a beauty. A compassionate new head came into the establishment with a soul and a conscience, who eventually reversed my suspension paying me all my withheld salaries to the glory of God. He is a God that truly never fails. The lessons of life's success are mostly hidden in the tribulations we encounter. In the first year in my hood, God had to equip me with the strength for the journey by allowing those things to happen because the experiences truly reinforced my zeal to overcome alone with God on the lead. The ejection taught me to depend on no one as it exposed me early to the harsh reality of my new world. The suspension gave me an opportunity to sort out my accommodation while saving the money in bulk which was very much useful when it came. The saying, there is a blessing in every disappointment may sound like a cliché but in reality it is true. When trials of life come and one's dream takes a nosedive, once you believe in God and keep to your purpose in faith as it becomes a drive through to the next level. Every experience I tell you has its benefits, if there is no material gain, there is a spiritual reward; the totality of result is the buildup of one's wholeness.

Widowed, Wounded and Whole

To be "widowed" is a deep bruise not just to the soul but to the entire being. In its pain, one is wounded as she goes through trauma in the struggle of survival; but being "Whole" is learning to see every experience as the resources for one's empowerment. It is our ability to learn that tribulations are resources that make us stronger and greater. I always believe that God can use devil himself to bless so when any help offer comes with humiliation and abuse, then for sure it is not God's. For He said His blessings do not add sorrow to it (Proverbs 10:22). Being "wounded" is not just the pain of his loss but the loss of you in the so many things one has to endure. The best way to deal with the circumstances is to trust God and work on yourself to live a life devoid of bitterness. Total trust in your God rather than man makes it easy for you to go through life in this hood with less pain. Often most people in your survival pursuit will want to capitalize on your situation to abuse one. They see ones need and therefore, paddle at the vulnerability of that need to bruise further your wounded soul. Muzzle up strength and throw away the pain by walking away. It can be frightening with the responsibilities you are handling but remember God has the best plan mapped out before creation. When wounded and your need becomes an object of ridicule; always refuse to give up by not giving in. In that you walk and work in "whole" to continue to strive. There are always two ways that are the best alternatives from God; a prayer and a step away. God will do it. There is going to be a lot of "beast" to encounter and be wounded, but we have the "beauty" of God abounding mightily to be whole. You may think that the battle is fierce because of what you are seeing or going through but be assured that what God is protecting us from are greater than your imagination.

It's nice to work carefully in our deal with widows; God is faithful to his words as he fights her battle. Yes, we can't get it all right, and God sees all hearts. He rewards all works from the heart as such sees all intention and purpose. We must pray always for God's forgiveness and the forgiveness of those we have wronged knowingly and unknowingly. Our actions are often out of weakness, with fatigue Will. With the emotions that are in constant battle, a widow has to deal with it in every of her actions and reactions. These are feelings that have most time led to misinterpretation of most innocent actions. If she's a family or friend, show more empathy in dealing with her, a whole lot of genuine friendships have been lost as a result of lack of understanding. Her pride can be in conflict with her rational reasoning especially having been abused most times. Truly, she needs all the support and advice as she often feels ashamed to ask for fear of being discussed in her wounded state. But to be widowed, wounded and whole is to live in hope, prayer and work with love to victory.

CHAPTER SIX
PRAYING OUT THE PAIN

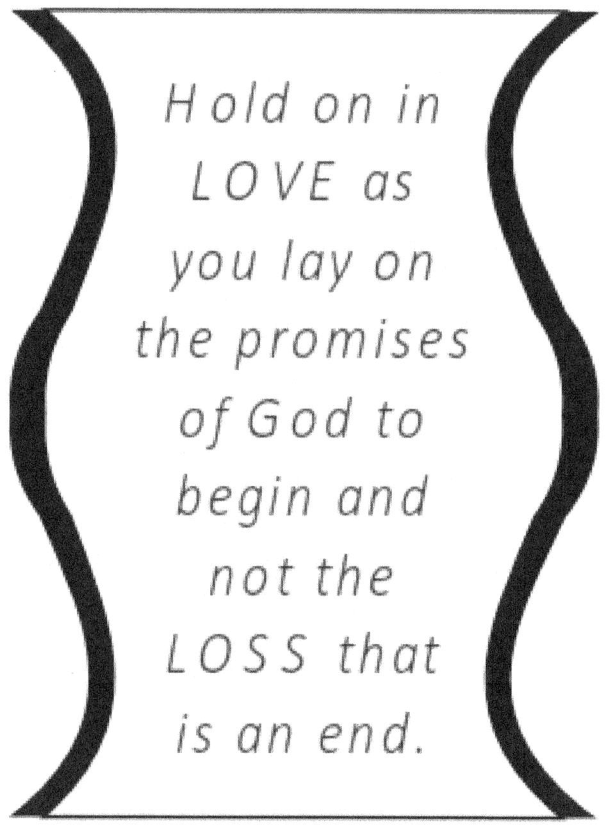

Hold on in LOVE as you lay on the promises
of God to begin and not the LOSS that is an end.

The pain of a widow is not in the death only; it is most times engraved in her heart by people through their words and deeds. People often see just that of her loss but it's more the sore of her wounded soul that comes with his death. There are always people who seem to have taken authority from the devil to inflict pain on a widowed woman either in words or deeds. I had one of such who swore that I would never have peace after my husband's death, believing that I needed to be broken further as my pain was well deserved. I cannot describe accurately the amount of torture and grief they added to my soul as my days and nights of lamentation increased. The increasing fear arising daily drove me to suicidal thoughts. But for God; the Words, mercy and the fear of God, my family would have been a part of the statistics. I remember thinking of the possibility of killing myself and my four children as I was not ready to die and leave them to suffer but saw that the task did not look an easy one to His grace. In fear, frustration and pain, wailing and praying one night, I remember asking God specifically to get these people off my back. I did have them off my back but I had to pray again all night reading all the Psalms as I saw God fighting my battle in them in a way that scared me to a point of compassion in their confusion. The trauma that beheld them, with problems that kept them too busy to remember me though; was disturbing to the point that I had to beg God for his peace to be restored to them all around as I had forgiven them. The Lord did this for me because they did not only have their problem solved then, but it made them forget me; giving me a peaceful relief. That was a wonderful introduction to me on the power of God in keeping to his promises as he says "Call upon me in times of trouble and I will answer you" (Psalm 50:15)

Widowed, wounded and want to be whole? God, he is faithful and just require us to seek, ask and knock constantly, never warring and He will deliver us. He has ability to make us see the beauty in these ashes. In all the painful feeling and with all the tears flowing, up the spirit of prayer with your work no matter how small the job seems without waver, the bigger one that will come. We must learn to overcome by not succumbing to what's happening around us and taking responsibility of our life with depending on someone do so for us. To be happy in the hood is possible; all it takes is to never get tired of moving forward in desires, hope and direction. Despite how you are being driven round, continue in your PUSH to PULL your hook in the hood. No matter how disheartened remember, it could have been worse. And when you want to give up the crown might just fall at the next pull. I have come to realize that in this journey, though God might seems to be saying "No" by not answering as desired, His "Yes" in that "No" is greater and with a far more exceeding goodness beyond our imagination whenever we pause to analyze the past.

If you want to discover this, stop complaining and compiling your needs and desires, rather, start counting and collating his deeds. You will see for truth that what God has done in all circumstances is greater in different ways than our expectations. When the heat of the hood emotions has melted away all one hope, just spin your last energy wheel to the simplest prayer as I, "Thank you Lord for all that I am. I need you still to become what I am to be; I can't do it but you will do it". In His coolness, you'll see all the waxes of hopelessness melted, congeal to hope with the energy not just to pray and the faith to fly but a rejuvenated spirit to continue the work. It is the "whole" that others behold. It shines with rays of brightness that renews one's daily strength, giving out the power of a smile that wins all circumstances that abound. In it lies all power to victory. The bad news in this "Whole" is that some seem irritated by it and feel it's a celebration of widowhood, as such, becomes unfriendly while others develop a lack of compassion in attitude.

In the midst of all the trials of any marriage, no one can truly wish for the death of the partner. I have never seen a woman that will willingly kill her husband except if the devil took her over completely as we hear on deliverance grounds and watch in movies. I am sure thereafter, their lives are full of regrets, as the pain, the grief, the shame and fear that will overtake her world is beyond her expectations. When you see a widow glowing, her victory is born out of all supporters, their actions, understanding of the grace of God. Her true strength and beauty seen in each smile is a determination to live on again. Don't be deceived or envious of the seeming glamour and vigor, often one really doesn't know how it grew out of all the strain except for the fulfillment of God's promise. And not even she can question such grace except one to unseat God. Don't ever feel she's joyous about her state, no one will be; happiness is a gift of God that come at the break of each dawn to all not excluding the widowed. She has learnt that widowhood is not a curse. There is absolutely no reason for a widow should not be victimized, segregated, abused, shunned, exploited, discriminated, omitted or unrecognized in the affairs of life; her life is her right given by God. Widowhood also is not a club, and should not be celebrated, admired, desired or envied.

Marriage is the most beautiful experience that should be enjoyed and not endured. Unfortunately, most widows miss it greatly, even in their public show of being good to be. In your marriage explore every opportunity to enjoy and never wish life can be better out of it; remember the grass seems greener on the other side. Behind that face you see shining with smile are conceal pain of loneliness. Don't ever feel she's happy with widowhood, she's only happy with her life. The abundance of her riches does not fill in totality the emptiness of her memories nor the voracious eyes of her world talk less of the cold nights of her life. Where does one start the tale, is it the physical and psychological abuse she have to accommodate or the emotional starvation and deprivation we fight to contain? You can never understand the pain if you are not in it. What you see is simply the happiness illuminating from above. She's learned to be contented in His works as she takes hold of her life with His promises. When feel the power to rob her off, be careful. All our words and actions to widows is measure by her creator. Remember, God is faithful to his words (Num 23: 19); he said that when you inflict pain on widows and they cry to him in prayer that he will make your wives widows and your children fatherless (Ex 22: 23-24).

Widows didn't lobby for it; I believed it because I have tested it. In pain, grieving and confused comes the feeling of total contortions that one often find oneself almost in an incomprehensible state and all we can do in that agony and confusion is to cry in prayers for help from above. In supplications, we ask for a relief of the anguish that we're drowning in. I tell you if you as a human being, were to see the wailing heart of a widow in that solitude, the magnitude of her fear, the excruciating pain in her the often humiliating shame of her loneliness, the amount of distress to her heart and the degree of wetness in her pillow, you are likely to be more brutal in your fight to protect her than God.

Dear widowed woman, whenever in despair and have finished all you know to do as lie in wait, all you need do in there is to continue in prayer to God because your pain evokes his sympathy. He is the only one, ever faithful and most reliably that is always awakes to answer us. In truth, we will not drive her to the state that will draw that wrath if we could just show a little compassion. The tiniest act of understanding can draw praise and thanksgiving.
"We beg not for your sympathy" "She prays only for your empathy".
From her world all she begs for is empathy because in God she'll have her sympathy. If we can before we act take a pause to imagine it in you. See? If you can't take it, don't dish it out. She is not as strong as assumed; it is an act of strength she is displaying to save her sanity. Likewise, why do it to her when you will loathe it on yourself? Though one seems to be taking it, it sure has the same taste to all mouths; she's merely forcing herself to swallow it all, just to be alive for her children.

The most crucial stage is the first three to five years. The rain in the Hood can come pouring without ceasing. There will abound deeds of fear and emotions of doubt. It goes from the fear of surviving to the pain of overcoming, through to the shame of the stigmatization and the grief of the loneliness. There are going to be different deeds for one to experience. It is going to be raining almost continuously that you will have to learn to contend with it by providing an internal shelter which helps you to contain the external through constant prayers. As you will be trying to internalize the situation to adjust, the external factors of the battle will most often make it harder if you allow it. More often than not, people, genuinely and unintentionally, will set a war path. Though some I believe will seem to be enjoying the act but there's a mistrust arising more from suspicious assumptions developed overtime by culture; as well as the her emotions. To the widow, it can start with the little things as; my husband did this or that in all the discussions by a friend that is like iodine poured onto an open skin to refusing to pick up your call. And you having male friends and associates asking you to undress on the slightest appeal for financial assistance. That's when you see that sex can be as cheap and expensive as a loaf of bread, depending on which side of the deal you are. "It is either you sleep with me or forget any assistance from me", very common statement to hear as a widow. It's very true it often goes with female gender but the vulnerability in widowhood places her out.

In praying out these pains, you have to decide to make yourself happy by making less use of your sense of hearing and feeling. Perfect the act of letting go of all what you see or hear without thinking deep through but putting it all into in prayer. The treatment a widow receives in our society all through her life cannot be told completely nor can it be exaggerated. I hear people ask, how did you survive? I often shred my shoulder. How can one translate the emotions to words so as to transmit the humiliation to you for you to really feel it to understand it? It is in a panoply of lives can it be possible to showcase the monsters of your actions that would have destroyed her. To most widows you see in their silence, they either find it difficult to get the words that can express it, too angry to relay it or too shameful to describe the state that they have been most time in order to keep their pride.

The pains in the struggle of survival are numerous. In as much as I love to take you through our world, I find the door very difficult to open as the rooms are cluttered with tales of deeds to which yours might be inclusive. If you are asking for the door, the question is; is the society willing to come through the thin line to see her world truly and for what purpose? Is it to change their attitudes of reject to that of social ingest towards widows? I am not sure of your purpose but one thing is certain, widowhood remains the most hidden and veiled area of violations of human rights and to unveil it is a decision of the society to which the traditional and religious leaders must lead not just in prayer but with actions as they move to get the government to provide social justice for women during widowhood with policies and facilities. But while we wait on this, be assured that it is only through each of our positive action can we begin the mend.

We all have friends and associates both male and female, but as soon as one husband dies they immediately change their perception of you. You immediately become a symbol; to most you are either an object of sex or a symbol of liability. As the female friends withdraw from you for fear of their husbands or their money, the male counterparts use you to satisfy their desire as they perceive you as a liability. I strongly believe that no assistance that you render to a widow will ever destroy your budget or project especially when there is no condition attached to it. When God wants to use you to fulfill his promises and you make yourself available to be used, I believe he has already made a double portion replacement that is exceedingly greater than you desire or imagine in return especially when you do not look for a reward. And to ladies that shield their husbands for fear, I respect that. But here the words of James Allen "man is made or unmade by himself, in the armory of thought he forges the weapon by which he destroys himself". I empathize with such women but believe in yourself, and reach out to the widow in faith and goodwill, God will always fight that battle if betrayed. Better still, you can even do the good work directly for the husband. I have personal and corporate friends who I occasionally send to tell their husbands to send my Christmas gift and in most cases they bring it. I remember saying so to one and with her response; I told her that I do not care how she would do it, you both are one. She smiled and left; and she later had delivered a bag of rice to me at Christmas.

Likewise as a widow, we need to be empathetic too, we need to think through and think twice before doing things to everyone around us. Always be cheerful and patient, don't let your spirit be sore and acrid; you must learn to understand and find good in both persons and actions. One of the things I do is to view and excuse all negative treatment as ignorance, it makes it less painful. There's nothing in widowhood both the good and bad that is a right. It is either a favor or a foul. There are truly some never happy widows who expect too much from the world. I have met some that are very unrealistic in their expectations. In praying out these pains one must consider the self-inflicted one. We must understand also that no one has too much to give both in cash or care. Human beings are created by God in such an incomplete state. It is only in the love of God and man that we can fill the gap where greed and jealousy looms. In order not to multiply our pain, we must understand that everyone has enough issues of their own in life as to go looking for others to join. If you have someone, friend or relative close to the family prior to his death you feel should help, make it a duty to inform them of your need or ask for assistance as meekly as possible with all your dignity. Sitting on the well-structured chair of pride and arrogance to complain of their lack of support is like getting married and living a celibate while going on dry fasting in prayers for the "fruit of the womb". One must work as God perfects.

When you have done your own by asking and is rejected or refused then you go away. But be satisfied and let the pain not sit in, just know that God has your name in his palm and so cannot forget you as not to see what you are going through; he obviously has his plan. I have seen widows out of pride in disguise go about grumbling yet refusing to inform relatives or friends on how they can be assisted. In life, the three basic principles of receiving remains seek, ask or knock; even in a lottery. You play; that's how every favor is received. You must seek to find. Learn to respect the situation of others. You cannot eliminate the pain if you are inconsiderate. I have male friends whose wives I have tremendous respect for so I choose not to be friends of their families. While the friendship remains personal in utmost purity, I maintain the corporate friends even in family gatherings especially having detected some act of insecurity from their women. One must learn to understand that life is not all about self. Let's not use our state as blackmail as some of us do. Show a lot more understanding to all, they too have their own emotions they are battling with.

In all encounter; no matter the magnitude, refuse to be angry and bitter, it destroys you more than any other. When you have prayed and whatever the result "God is aware". I remember saying to a widow friend in one of those occasions, when in her devastation and seemingly hopeless situation she was raining all curses on a family friend whom she had run to in one of her greatest times of need, crying, praying and pleading for his assistance. He did promise and on the agreed day, though in the office told the personal assistant not to welcome her with the reason of him not being available. The obvious look of the Personal Assistant as he delivered the message so humiliated her further. I know the story because I have been there uncountable times. Genuinely, you could reject the assistance without raising her hope or when you cannot meet up the promise for reasons known to you, welcome the appointment with an apology of another day. When so done, even without the assistance, it leaves a greater sense of dignity she leaves to continue in hope.

Most often as widow you can decode the reality of the promise. If there's a condition no matter how subtle he comes, there's very much likely the promise was a "bait" to increase the condition. I learnt to either ignore the appointment or go with just a mere chance of God's miracle. This makes the result either a testimony or a big joke. As Ann said, "I had to contend with the issue of a very junior colleague of my late husband who was in a position to help me with a Local Purchase Order (LPO). He had earlier in my bereavement appeared truly willing to assist and with all encouraging attitude. When he started in between the business to demand for an amorous relationship, in my shock and humiliation I confronted him and after that day he cancelled the deal while shutting the door against my visit as he terminated the friendship."

With the broken heart and shattered hope from the loss of the deal, comes the despondency. What do we do? Yes, in weeping and raging, channel your anger and pain to God in prayer, after all He knows why he chose to "kill our husbands" if you think so. But you'll agree that in the midst of our pain, He still gives great room for His praise and benediction. Understand that in men exist the problems of desire and lack; we are all living with it. In their promises and rejections they might be battling with their own lack. It's either the Will or the material to give as well as the desire of selfishness that has to be met. As we battle with the emotions of our widowhood so do they battle with their emotions of lack and desire in their own manhood even the women also. We all need God's grace to help us live a life of love and care for others in all circumstances.

GOD'S ABUNDANCE IN ALL

A true analogy of the power of God's abundant life in all situations was made manifest in an experience I encountered years ago. I, bereaved of my husband, as I got that title "a widow", the feeling and task associated with this indescribable journey of confusion, rejection, dejection, depression is crowned with loneliness as I sat in my home looking through my world wide open. I had a friend of mine; fortunately her husband did not die only bed ridden from a car crash, a "vegetable" as he was referred to then, existing more than living.

One of those days in my loneliness I decided to pay Mary a visit. In getting to her home, there abide a few people that had come to comfort her. Further discussion revealed to me that she gets such regular visits and assistance from friends, church and relatives. To my surprise I realized how for a moment I had longed to trade places as I could not remember the last time I had such visit. My encounter that day taught me a great lesson. Looking at our two conditions, I realize we both have reasons to be grateful to God for there were blessings in our two conditions. It gave me a truly new lesson in life of God's omniscience and how he makes it my abundant in all situations. I saw the beauty of God on us, while I can thank God for not giving my husband such pain and myself such burden as I was relieved of the burden of a helpless husband so also could Mary as; she is replenished with the comfort and care of all who come regularly in love to support.

In these two lives of ours, apart from the eternal comfort of abundant life that comes from loving God, there is the physical provision that Christ has personally given to each of us through a leverage of joy and hope, making both of us to agree truly there is a blessing in each situation; if only we can look to see it. All we need to do in any circumstance is to find a source of joy and enjoy it rather than allowing the devil to keep us in the bondage of unhappiness with the picture of the worst of it in that position. Whenever we do so, we make him delay or destroy our future.

IT IS FINISHED, YET JUST A BEGINNING

Yes, the death of my husband brought an end to a begun life, yet it is a start to the beginning of a similar life but with a different altitude. It can be a whole beautiful one even though I never thought or believed so at his death. It is all dependent on our choices. There's certainly a chance to be taken but we often get fixated to the plan that ended. The death of Christ was never in the plan of his followers but it tore the veil in the temple making God more accessible through grace. This means that our dreams are still accessible in his death. I learned to make a choice taking my chances by looking through the veil than the void. The loss of his presence is a void but there's still the fullness of my vision. As a widow, I am looking unto Jesus the author and finisher of our faith should be more in our attitude than intellectual understanding or declaration. It is simply knowing to leave his end and focus on His begin.

In that you should not only have hope, but you learn to feel love and experience peace through faith. God said he has plans of good not of evil... to bring us to future hope (Jer 29: 11). Allowing one's husband to die does not seem like a plan of good, I did not only think but, I said so. Balancing my situation with that promise was not easy initially, but I got there in time simply by learning to count my fortune more than the pains and its woes; the greatest being always my life. As I constantly ask myself this in each intense pressure; how have I been doing it alone? Irrespective of the seemingly darkness, do not be deceived; life could be worse. In time, I have learnt that no matter how dark or scary to thank God for life so far as I pray to him to complete it. We have to seek to see a vision of the new mission by letting go of the past. We still have the purpose to achieve and the potential to do so and lamenting on would have is devil's act in holding us hostage. We must begin again for God with all the divine helpers waiting to lead us. So recognize that all the devil wants is to make you miss them by placing his obvious which is the loss. Whenever the negative is placed before you; be it in person, practice and position, that holds you in the agony of his death, let it go. Often we feel we must stay there so as not to lose him but his gone already.

You must understand that he left to end a journey, leaving a beginning of another to which you have the authority to decide its direction. We must arise in positive. We don't have the good but the best; it's a new journey. Though very difficult to explain but "easy to feel" once you grow the attitude. Don't feel responsible of making family and friends know you still love by holding to everything that you will keep him. It is painful and confusing but in that muddled feelings of despondency remains a hope that the tears cannot wash away, which is a door to begin anew. Activate the hope by aligning to God fulfill your own mission in this new life with gladness even in the grey.

While our love song Lionel Richie Destiny said "you are my destiny", oh I love this and we rocked it well; yet it will never dispute my saying "You are your destiny" especially now that our destiny has end. So even as you begin, in the darkest condition when you will fail; falter, faulted and fall, but arise, amend and begin in prayer looking up without dwelling in shame as you work on in the walk. Each end is a beginning; keep using the card by surrendering to that glimpses of hope lighted to you at every end, no matter how little. Grace said, no not after I've been through ma, when my husband died everything in me died. Nothing worth holding on to. I wake up and ask if life will ever having a meaning to me again. Will this pain ever end?

Begin again is the code to overcome at last. Look always to God; the beginning and the end master. Believe in his unmerited grace and begin if you want to get to your expected future at each. When you look unto man they have an end that will either disgrace or discourage you. It's either they will be pointing out the impossibilities of your situation or the worthlessness in your station. Some people can tell in joy that certain things are not at your disposal. A widow went to a family friend for assistance, the wife asked, "How can your child and mine be in the same school and you are looking for our assistance". This woman's plan with all her pain since the husband's death was to take her children to another school once the academic session is ended but the friend thought otherwise. She came out angry and humiliated, what do she do? Think about it and be bitter? Know end the thought and begin away and look for a solution.

A widow may have to move from a flat apartment to one room and move her children from their schools to cheaper ones; basically a lot of remodeling of life must be done to put an end to certain things so as to begin anew. These are logical actions a widow will sit down to plan, decide and take action after the husband's death and anyone relatives or friends that have genuine advice must put themselves in that condition and prayerfully pick the place, time and condition to do it not the day she comes for your assistance. Timing and caution should simply be taken and considered in doing so, knowing that to begin can be easy but to end an abrupt end like a life of a married women who wakes up to see herself a widow is not any easy one. In reality, it never ends it just neatly tucked away in a locked box of our lives to be opened at each our kids' milestone achievement.

A widow's good friend should make out time, knowing the woman's weaknesses and strengths advise her on how they can help or what can bar her from successfully carrying out any of her new mission. It is so appropriate when your friend comes asked for your assistance to give the advice, let's face it; it will certainly be taken as "is it because I came?" If you have seen this as a friend shouldn't you have advised me earlier on? It can lead to the interpretation of you rejoicing in her misfortune waiting for her to fail so you can call her a failure because of her emotional state. Weak and illogical it may seem, if she comes to ask, as much as you can, make the pain less hurting in your approach. Even if you don't have say so, though it can be doubted God knows it all. Her emotion is often in turmoil and will fight the noblest deed to futility deepening her shame and widening her fear. In this, the feeling of rejection and depression increases. She has an end fighting so hard to conquer in order to embrace wholly to her new beginning.

Once a woman loses her husband her emotions most times are torn between the life of the end and that to begin. She has the fear of what has to be done or will be done to her and shame of how to do it best. While she drowns in on who will be there and the pain of all what she is seeing and feeling, learning to accept the beginning takes a whole lot of effort. When Adam in the Bible called her the bone of my bone and flesh of my flesh, (Genesis 2: 23), it is true. His death takes something away from you that cannot be explained nor ever can be replaced. It brings an end to one part of you. You feel completely naked with all your clothing on, there is an irreplaceable void created in your soul that makes you feel the least in most of your senses. "Fully dressed, yet naked" There is an emptiness that nothing is ever able to fill but for the spirit of God. He knows the end from the beginning and knew about his end. Just know He has the right cloth for that nakedness. Often we think there's a stipulated time to accept to end. But I tell you it's best to close that end as quickly as you can and begin the beginning without fear of future by not looking into it but the future. I was told by a widow who in crying for her husband's death kept saying "God why didn't you keep him alive and let him continue to beat me". It is an unacceptable practice for a man to beat his wife, very inexcusable and dehumanizing, but you can see from the battered wife that the pain and humiliation for such a woman cannot be likened to that of widowhood. Even in his death, she couldn't even accepted its end, instead prayed to accept more battering in its place.

Yes, the death of strips you of your crown and its glory replacing it with feathers of shame. There is no silver lining as you look because the end of that tunnel cannot be seen especially at his death. You need to see the end to begin you'll say of the tunnel. Our fear initially lies most in the bleakness of the future, with the shame of all the questions; while our pain bound in the loneliness of the state as we grieve the uncertainty of an end. The job is difficult for the power of two, how possible then when reduced to one. The children, shelter, feeding, fees, the loving even the fighting; the list is unending but to begin leave fear that's in the future begin with today, at the end of today begins tomorrow. To you, try to add up her duties for the future if you can; may be then will you be able to understand and appreciate the magnitude of her emotion; may be you'll able to feel her in empathy rather than in sympathy. The pride in my dignity, my crown and the glory of my womanhood; taken away over a night unexpected, unprepared and unapproved. At his death her walls were shattered. As you look through 'A Widow's Window, do you see how her world is thrown open and everyone cannot only look into her life, but will most often than not feel, talk and can act as desired with no regard on her living or respect for his death?

For most widows' apart from battling with the mental pride, most of our cultural practices, though being fought against today by most religions and the culture itself are faced with a lot of undignified statement, treatment and action especially from her fellow women starting from the very day of the death. Some in-laws, friends, business associates even employees have robbed the woman of her pride of place. Imagine an in-law coming to a woman to ask for the car keys, bank books, office key and landed documents to the point of fighting physically for it in the presence of the children. This is a woman with children and has invested her life and strength in her home. Even her juniors are at will with authority to talk to her as desired. Just the previous day she was the madam in her home and all these under her courtesy of her husband. Even in a home in crisis her pride of place is intact as no one can walk into her home to do that when the man is there to provide the cover. But his death immediately opens all, that even the dearest family and friends can freeze you in shock with their action. Where are you in this as you've looked?

The picture is horrific and it makes the end more painful, yet it is the entire end to the beginning, so end as quickly as you can and begin again. Janet said, my in-laws has taken everything from me living me and kids with nothing, how can I end it? Where do I begin? Our culture and society is wicked to this deed. With court it will not end. The cost you can't manage and the corruption will overpower you. Unfortunately the husband complicated issues by not tiding up papers. So you must end by moving forward. Start at you point, in time the kids will ask them the questions that the court may never asked them. In all these, the best attitude in this beginning for quicker recovery is to flush out all thoughts, deeds and objects of pain even if it means remaining you, your children and your job. Begin light by losing the crowd and there with only your God. Assuredly, later when you are settled and stronger they will all come back in a better state. Then will you be able to process all thoughts as a testimony, their deeds as the dividend, all mess as the message; as victory becomes the wires of your benediction making it their rendition. Be not ashamed of anything but pride trust in God as you move on. He is so mighty in the battle and will give you your winning cord. Do not let any state in the journey to overwhelm you. No matter the degree their humiliating treatment or your failure, end at each end to begin. Nothing can be more than this said Betty. She is so right. The climax of the state is with the installation of that title, a "widow" by his death. Absolutely nothing can be worse than his death.

"I remember my 12 years daughter warning me sternly pointing to my face "don't ever let me hear you call yourself that thing". This was simply on her hearing my formal conversation with a friend on the telephone, jokingly saying to him that God will ask him how he has been caring for the widow He left in his care. The intensity of her disgust to that name was powerful, it could be seen and felt because after asking her for the third time what thing, she maintain, "that thing you called yourself" she never mentioned the word with her mouth. That's an idea of the disgust and shame that is associated with that position that even a young girl of 12 years found it so undignified a title for anyone to call her mother talk less of her calling or addressing her mother thus. But my only comfort and pride in it all remains our position is part of God's plan, "till death do the part". He knew. He has the cord dropping down at that end. Grab it to begin by leaving the end, there's still great abundance ahead. As a young widow He has liberated us to remarry while taking absolute care of us in the interim and even as an old widow he has positioned us to the church for care and service. The question is how well is the church doing in the ministry to its widows and what help are they rendering in the service?

CHAPTER SEVEN

RE-MARRIAGE

In widowhood, the pain of loneliness and the fear of all that is around one will more often than not push you against the doctrine of your faith, but once you believe in your soul of God's sovereignty and existence, that is your first step of faith. Communion and followership with His Word sharpens all other tools as He empowers you the Holy Spirit to you. It is in God's comfort that you can daily improve into a better being.

With children I did not talk about the issue of re-marriage except on a few occasions when I tried to tease them about it and I noticed that the older two who knew their father very well and had a close relationship with him, were not open to the discussion. I did nurse the prospect of re-marriage and discuss it with friends in similar situations from time to time even though I wish above all for God's perfect will to rule in my life". Yes, and I believe it is part of His will. The Bible makes it clear "till death do us part", with the shock and pain the decision of marrying again remains an individual thing but all consideration of the children must be taken. The issue of loneliness in widowhood is real. When the children are young, there is so much work that keeps one busy. The physical exhaustion with its distraction drowns the desire a little bit, yet emotional sensuality evokes the emotion quite often.

This resurfaces more for the younger widows which becomes deepened when the kids are grown. As they leave home to start their own lives the issue of companionship becomes eminent. The greatest challenge for younger women is the sexual desire and warmth of a hold, no matter how hard you work around it in silence; its numbness is often temporary as it remains a great battle in the pursuit of God's Kingdom as regard to holiness. Though we all deal with this differently, some are stronger while most are weaker. And as Paul said, it is better to marry than to burn with passion. (1Cor.7:9b). As a widow you'll never wake up to have your man lying beside you even if it means not talking to each other, talk less of saying "NO". Those nights of his discomfort as a wife becomes a luxury to which you can never afford or enjoy. In wanting to save the soul, the spirit being; God knows that the body has its needs, among the basic one are love and sex.

Paul in his epistles made it clear, don't force yourself or be forced. If you cannot, go and marry. And in keeping to that, the marriage was maintained till death do thee part. It further instituted the widows of the church to be sixty years of age. We need the church to help open this culture also. There is a conspiracy of silence in the church when it comes to addressing the issues of widows as regard her sexual need. As the day is dawn and darkness descends ones greatest prayer always is that the almighty will send his sleep angels to rock you to sleep since there is no man in the house, so that you do not indulge in the memory of the past; what it was or when will it ever be it again? No wonder the Bible truly had different category age of women in widowhood (1 Timothy. 5: 9, 14). In His goodness He has created the freedom by saying "till death do us part" in the marriage vow. I realize that most of us have engrossed ourselves with what people will say or is expected of us that we forget to pray or desire for a husband thereby not getting one while languishing in the silence of loneliness. We must learn to take up courage and live not to conformity. Though the biggest challenge is the inability of the society to address it from the root.

God said he will give you the desire of your heart; most widows in their youth never did any of these. We are most afraid of others more, than the concern for ourselves. The pain of loneliness is far greater than the fear we have of what will be our thought. From the start of our journey, our concerns were either of the children or the society, as we envelop our lives with what I call the "Great Expectations", where we have every one's own excluding ours. We are expected to be a loving faithful wife even in his death for us to be valued. Young widows I believe should include the desire for another loving relationship in their prayer request among others though that notwithstanding, we should relinquish everything to be done according to God's will as we take absolute care of the children he had put in our custody.

My advice to young widows is to start as soon as possible to address the issue of re-marriage yourself expecting no one to hail you. The later it is, the more complicated it gets as the issues of relinquishing your freedom after getting too independent, too comfortable yet too lonely becomes more fearful. Also getting your desired status to the children becomes a greater barrier with the greatest barrier being that of our culture where our matured adult male singles are looking for their daughter's friends as companions. The issue of re-marriage should be taken into consideration by a young window as soon as possible. We should frown at the culture that discourages it in actions and expectations. We have been made indirectly to see ourselves not suitable for marriage once widowed no matter how young, especially where children are involved. Imagine as young widow of 27 years refusing a 37 years old suitor that am not right for him. I tell you, the rejection was born out of my fear in what culture will think, say or even do. I knew the rejection I will face from the suitors family, so I rejected it myself instead.

This is even worse in the eastern part of my country. One cannot bear to imagine what a mother will tell her son even a 40 year old who takes home a 25 years old widow. Most parents especially women will gladly accept a 40 years old spinster instead. The residual effect of our widowhood practices and rites across our Nigerian culture has made it that even a young widow without children will fight a battle of acceptance with the family of a new suitor. The most painful aspect of this is the widow not understanding how messed up her ideology is as she ascertains herself unfit to marry. Adaeze is a young widow in her early thirties. She said "When my husband died, I met a man who has lost his wife though they had no children and we started dating. Few years later even though he suggested that we get married, I refused. I encouraged him to go and get a wife" because like she said I have seven children and people will say "I have cage him under my spell with voodoo". She supported this man whom she confessed taught her what love and sex really mean to a woman to marry as they remain secret lovers.

In time as expected it broke out and she was made a mockery of by her church Pastor. She sent an opportunity of remarriage away herself to choose to be mistress because society has made her see herself as such with the Pastor taking a position of condemnation, where they are not contributing in teaching the Bible stand loud enough to the hearing of the congregation to acculturate.

I have the incident of a woman telling her 25 years daughter to go and adopt a baby boy after the death of her husband. Why? To retain a position in family she married into. In a culture where property is bequeathed only to the male child, her mother a United State trained; acting subconsciously from the effect of this cultural manipulation believed that her daughter cannot either be expected to remarry or will not see a man that will want to marry her again. This is a marriage that lasted barely four years. So if she goes to adopt a son to add to her four daughters; for who, for what and for how long? If she is to live the 70 years of the Bible designed age with the grace which we all pray for even more years as Christians, that is over 50 years of loneliness, with her median age love, romance and sex completely taken away from her as she battles with religious principle and practices. How is she going to raise her daughters in pride if she continues to change her dates, as will certainly be her lot under such circumstances? Hiding in a self-deceit of Christianity hardly takes away the demon of loneliness especially at such prime in youth, as some have even worsen their state by dethroning the sacredness of men of God as they sleep together.

Our society needs re-orientation with women taking the lead. It is absolutely an abuse for a married woman as I hear tell widows "what are you talking about remarriage; stay for your children. My question to such is why are you still with your husband when you have finished having kids? Kick him out if marriage is just for having children. As widows, we need to say it out to encourage each other. What is holding you from remarriage? Please let's learn to be honest with each other of our choices and its resultant effect. The men, they can't complain they are most in gain to the situation. A relationship that is not concrete is bound to collapse because it is not yours. I call it sneaking and stealing, you can never have a life of love in full nor enjoy it with pride in liberty; they all add to the shame to which we bear as most often the conflict of guilt and satisfaction results to distaste.

This is what we most often go through and sometimes settle for. We have to decide to change most of our culture especially we women as too much unfair expectations are imposed on us. The widow concentrates on her children once in the hood, excellent but the widower immediately goes for our daughters for replacement at his loss. As a young widow the earliest you decide to marry the better because in that, you have chances of getting someone suitable to your status chronologically in age and socially related. Refuse to be ashamed of the feelings and the act of doing so. We all should let go of the guilt feeling and ask God for the new beginning, seek a second chapter of love and marriage; he can give us out to be wife again. Don't be deceived by the luxury of the freedom. They are a trap we most get stuck especially as young widow as you dictate no nonsense limit you will take from any man; after all it is so easy to get him out life than the tight rope of marriage.

To remarry as a widow one must embrace herself and begin to desire it in reality to pray and work towards it. The negativity of our thoughts is often so toxic and often kills any seedling of love at its germination. Don't also be caught up with that man, who finds in convenient for him to sneak in. He is great but soon will retire to his closet. Yes, be happy, I know but with reorientation and remarriage we can be happier in a long last. Remarriage, God can make it work for our good but we need to address our perception and belief. With this we can modify our culture after all; culture is a way of life made possible by its people.

In a usual counselling, Nnenna asked "remarry? Well that will be after the graduation of my last baby". I laughed so hard that she couldn't help but ask what she said wrong. My dear sixteen years ago I said this to suitor on his proposal "you have to wait till my last kids graduate from the university" and that is after my recovery from a senseless laughter at his proposal. Angrily he walked away and out of my life with his friendship. It's one of the biggest fools I have ever made of myself. Not the refusal, because I was really attracted to him, so we weren't dating but friends as I kept turning off his advances. He obviously must thought that I will see his seriousness with that proposal. But in time I realized my main reason wasn't just the kids; behind it was the ideology of my culture. What will I say to my family and how will they perceive me. I tell you, in the dilemma of that phrase "your children" you stay only for them to grow out, as your friends grows in to their homes to understand the real reason for marriage; companionship. But then, when we have stayed for as long as expected by people to understand, and our class retire to their homes for companionship and our children grows out to start their own lives we are left alone to remember most past choices with regrets of all we could have done differently.

Some of us that waited till the children are all grown up and gone; not bad. Not bad at all, but what we see is that, having stayed to raise the children and give them away in marriage, we all have two obstacles that make it more difficult as well as the society advancing their opinion. There is the problem of being too independent to be a wife despite the desire for a companion. If we are not afraid of ourselves not knowing how to be a wife, the men are afraid of us, as the mature suitable widowers or even divorcees that nature must have made for widows will come but not for them but our daughters who are their daughter's mates because the culture of child bride isn't a crime with the societal decadence where money answers all things have refined relationship. Most parents especially mothers, today have no issue giving out their daughter's hand in marriage to their grandfather's age mate as long as he's rich; while some young boys who out of laziness has chosen fast route are willing to be paid to serve the older women. As a young widow don't waste your emotion of love and happiness on the fear of what people will say if you remarry like most old widows have done.

Stop living in the conformity of people's expectations; make hay while your sun shines. When you are in search for a companion in middle age, you will not go for their sons. Even if you can it will attract more gossip and worst still, it will bring a more awkward feeling for the children especially in our culture. The re-marriage is more honorable and will be better accepted in our society than the cougar system and the earlier we begin to cut the cord of those strings that amalgamated from our cultural practices and belief the better for us as a society. Our children will find it easier to learn to respect a real father figure as a stepfather than a mate figure in place.

When you want to make the choice, be assured in your fear that it can only be a story for a tale; which will ease with time as one glory in dignity when it becomes a culture like every other practice, as it is in most cultures. The children who remain our concern and most of the time our fear, when they become adults will definitely understand as long as one continues to love them in words and deeds. When we in our motherly love perform our responsibilities to them in wholeness, they will respect and accept our action. Besides you don't want to be a burden of worry for them while trying to make their own homes. They want to know you are happy and safely protected when they leave. Imagine a widow friend of mine, soliciting with the son that wants to marry to please do so but that they should still live in her house. That must be a big burden on the son, his saying 'yes or no' is going to hurt either of the two women he loves dearly. The love of a man cannot be replaced by that of a son; they have two separate channels to run in a woman's vein with none ever superseding the other, rather they are absolutely complementary. It is much more difficult to run the Christian, even the moral race as a young widow because of the issue of holiness; though not impossible to conquer will remain a battle.

The silent approach from the churches in preaching remarriage on the pulpit as a sermon is a disenfranchisement to young widows in most of our culture. When she's drained with those feeling tiredness, that's more than enough load on one individual and it often cause her to falter. It is misleading to think that there's a difference in weight between her lack of food in the kitchen and lack of sex in the bedroom. I tell you, tears flow more for the lack of a companion because there's power in sharing a problem. God in his perfection created the man with a helper, as a woman she's wired to be a helpmate so she is fashioned the strongest but yet in weakness. A widow can be the superwoman to all in all but the touch of her softness is still in the hole, so to be whole; you need to decide for you not for them by listening to your spirit where the comforter abodes. Happiness stems with achieving what you want, one must keep this in mind and search deep inside for the truth. Every tiniest desire of yours will magnify in age as kids grow out and friends grow in, that song that says "if I know back then what I know now" is a phrase common to widows in widowhood 301 all because of the choices they took in Widowhood 101 as the journey through Widowhood 201 in confusion.

CHAPTER EIGHT
THE POWER OF MENTORING

Side by side or miles apart, we wear and walk with a she; though sizes and steps differ yet our paths remain

The greatest prayers and support for one another should be our stories and testimonies. It is in another widow's story that a despondent one gains the strength which is the support she is looking for. It is the advice she is seeking and the hope she sees to begin. I make it a point of duty to share my true stories with any widow I meet whether she is a friend or not. In so doing, we become friends in care. This is my story, her story that is mostly our story. The stories are different yet similar, if you have not failed, you have fallen, if you have not faltered, you have faulted. That's all she needs to hear and that's what she wants to know so also is what the world is eager to see. Yes, the truth is absolute, in the tribe of widowhood lack is eminent; it is there in her economic, social and emotional journey. If you find it in all, you must see it in one. As sisters, don't be ashamed to share the total package of the hood experience with each other. It is not alone experience, we each have been there at different times, it's just the degree that varies.

Be a mentor, let's encourage one another. Are you newly widowed? As a mentee, seek a mentor in humility. Learn by asking questions. So many things will overwhelm you but in analyzing the pain; place it in between you purpose and potentials. Something in the result will put you in a place that will bring you joy to ignite your hope. True, so many friends will disappoint, even some will expect you're entitled to a lesser life but the choice you've taken determines the extent of authority you'll exhume. But be assured, when you refuse to be humiliated and abused, most will watch you in expectation to see the failure. As they wait and wish for it, don't be scared to step out even if you fall God is able is able to raise you. I was told I did not need a flat rather I should move into "a bedroom" apartment with my children. I didn't fret much, I only agreed in my soul that I can never go below; rather it will be beyond my husband's vision. Even in my pain and tears, my purpose motivated me to persevere to overcome. Though you can never be able to compare scores in achievements of the "end" to the "begin", which basically isn't a motive of competition but that of motivation and the results of each progress will keep you in the right direction.

Widowhood is a story of fear, pain, shame and grief. In it is loneliness as you commune physically alone in the solitude of world "within" to which the world in their "without" scrabble in thought to create their story. The story of women in widowhood is a dark glossy wall that the work of God illuminates in the brightness of His grace. I often ask this question, in her well looking you watch and in her ill looking you watch. Can you ever see what you are looking for? It is not pride but the zeal of hope in her to survive that you are seeing in her gloss neither is it shame when she looking sad; they are all part of her ride. Be it known to you, I begged my bragging, she faltered in her firmness and we faulted in our feebleness. No one wants to fail in this my walk, we just work continuously with our Will. I need the strength and so does she.
Have you not ever had an experience in failing? Yes, quit your imagination, the mortal being in her still exist, it never exited with his death. How much perfection do you expect in her?

It is often the fullness of the pleasure from those who give us the beauty experience though most times is of great scarcity in our supply that God multiplies her strength. In her daily life like manner, we collect it. Trying hard in each of the days to conquer but what you contribute most often can be painful. The society often in their action either give you fear in place of favor, pain in the name of pleasure or grieve to replace your ease. Often you are giving her shame that will overshadow her pride and make one sing blues. But learn to be a great self-cheerleader; in time you will overcome. Make the Lord your boss and friend in the lone career of widowhood. Yes the story are the same, I was not only abused but did bring some abuse in my despondency. As we struggle for social justice learn to be a "widow's sister ". It is being available to a next widow with your storyline covering the absolute experience. The greatest injustice you can do as widow is lying to one another. When you lie to another widow and make her feel that it is all rosy with you, her shame increases as she wonders in her fear 'why is my own different, have I sinned beyond pardon'? With her heart in dismay and her soul in despair her pain increases and in lamentation she grieves even more. Help her in keeping the faith to the race. Let her know that in the midst of that glamour lies also that feeling of worries and emptiness that defines the loneliness; the decisions and desires one fight daily with the often failures, the insecurity still covered in that beautiful surroundings and the uncertainty of what next with the fear of what will be tomorrow.

Yes, let her know they are all in the walk to each work even though it's been handed all to God, one still have to live through them daily. The only strength is that we no longer allow them to be in control as God is carrying them all making the weight much lighter. Don't be caught up in the spiritual blackmail. Yes, though I have my Bible beside me yet I cuddle my pillows in my cold times; I know very well how to pray and understand its power but my strength most times fails me in doing so; and though I am seen to be full of smiles, my nights can most times be grey as tears wet my pillows. But one thing we must know how to do well in this Hood is to live in the HOPE that God is good and His goodness is sure to come meet us at the valley. If it isn't today, it sure will be tomorrow and it is in that you live joyfully today in order to see tomorrow. It's a struggle of focus that one must leave every sadness of the past behind to face the present one before you. Let it be known to her that each one has travailed in the quest to survive.

I remember visiting a widow friend one day after a long time. In our discussion as she was telling me her stories and l gave her the examples, I felt her heart as it lightened until she truly got me deep into her pain. The shame in her as she said that she had no food at home only a warmed up stew of three days which the son is avoiding to eat again by pretending not to be hungry at about 2'O clock in the afternoon, with no breakfast. As I gave her a little money out of the small on me since I had fuel in my car to drive home and I said to her, 'my dear, I have been there a billion times' I saw the relief right in her soul. This is very true because as I watch her write little bit of everything to make soup and stew saying, 'thank God I can swallow today I remembered one of my experiences. It was one faithful Tuesday morning. I had no food on the table with no money to purchase either. In my despair, I went to early morning church service. After the service, I was torn between the shame of how and who do I present this my absolute lack and the fear of being disappointed, the Holy Spirit directed me to one mama. "Good morning ma, I said. Ma, please I need your assistance; I have no food at home and no money. I don't know, but please can you help me I continued fidgeting. After telling her the truth of not having money or food to feed my children and paused. Looking at me she said, I have nothing but a church committee envelop of N5,000 ($14.00) which I am to pass to the society treasurer. Looking at the envelope, she decided there and then and handed it over to me.

Almighty God I thank you, with thanks and tears in my eyes as I collected it, I rushed to the market buying little bits of soup, stew ingredients and other food stuff that will last a few days for my children and I. To Mama Lawani, "I thank you forever; your daughters will never be widows at young age as they will enjoy their marriage to a very good old age. I pray God Almighty to raise a world of helpers for them before they are in need". The greatest joy of that experience is, after our sharing as I was leaving her home, she said to me "Hope, thank God for your visit, you have given me hope that things will change" Though it's more of a question than a statement. "Yes" I replied, it will change I stated and in continuation I said your car is parked you cannot repair it, use the bus and motorbike because I have done so before for months. No condition is permanent. The only permanent condition is God's position and his promises. Just place your faith in His ability and keep your thoughts focused on your mission. Like an architect, draw dream mansions in your vision, when all hope seems lost don't just look at the castle move into it and live the life of your dreams. That will not only restore your hope, it will give you the power of victory over all obstacles of each day as you continue to look up to Him the author of this our memoirs knowing for sure that He as a bestselling author of all times is writing the story for tomorrow and the story we must win. (Heb. 12:12). Just keep your faith in the power of time; God will not only help you build the castle but will live permanently there with you, making sure that as you give your testimonies they will look more like a fiction even with all the truth shouting out to sight.

Just learn to let an end be and begin again at each end to end it yourself; let no one give you their end. Always remember, amid the happy well-made face and life, financially, everyone have had their downcast and often been confronted by some humiliating states; which had caused them to act in ways though not too proud yet happy in its sharing as they have built up a wealth of strength off it to which we are winning on. It is worthy of mentioning that in situations of loneliness and devastation of the hood, I have sometimes failed in my faith. Yet, despite my frailness I simply refuse to give in to my failures. You just have to be determined to make the life race of success in spirit, soul and body moving continuously in the direction of improvement with hope; smiling as often as you can despite the pain.

When the body fails, will up the spirit. It is only the joy that is in the hope of the future in which we are living that others will see to admire. As a widow, your greatest ability remains your faith. With faith as tiny as a mustard seed you can truly move mountains (Luke 17: 6). I have to ask myself this question, what then do you think will happen when you grow your faith big as an elephant? I tell you it is better experienced than imagined. Faith is a weapon of warfare in the journey of widowhood, faith it will get better; the vitamin of each day's success. Like me, you need to come to agreement with self that God will see you through. I had a hand-written card "my God will see me through" placed on my dressing mirror those days to which I see as I see myself at least every morning and night, till the day my first daughter came back from church after her graduation and changed the 'will' to 'has' and 'see' to 'seen'.

We grew an elephant size seed of faith that made it possible that no matter what it is, even in tears, with so much fear and uncertainty; I was resolute it will come to pass, and for sure it always does. In terms of overcoming the reproach of widowhood, having a 'desperado hope' helps in expanding your faith but be mindful always that it is not by anyone's power (Eph. 2:9), and be thankful to God always for his sufficiency and learn at each end to end to begin. Staying in a failed state with regrets can be a common experience as you sort to see find what you could done differently to avert it but moving on is the best. It is sure going to take time, determination and perseverance, but be assured to get it in time once you start. I have cried beyond imagination, disheartened as never can be explained, scared almost to death but in all, no matter how excruciating the pain, I cling to that tiny faith within which grows as the mustard seed indeed. We all have our tunnels in the loss, the valleys most times are too deep but I choose to look beyond at each time and behold at each dark hole is a light; the silver lining. It is that gaze at tomorrow and the dreams that magnets the hope. In it is that place of glory and the smile that shines out a light in you that others will love.

Be sure the darkness in the hood is scary, but when one's eyes are seeing it, and your ears hearing it, do not let your mouth confirm it. Always say what you want, not what you are seeing or hearing. The power of spoken words is true and is more than enough to destroy all that is seen and heard. Pray for the grace to use your desire in words more; not your sight. Frankly it works, most positive things I have said in my worst conditions which ordinarily in sight was impossible to achieve by me were heard by God, which I am even surprised it is happening. It is one of the simple work I tell widows to do. "Say what you want and not what you see". Our children can be our mentor too, listen to them and take their words. God uses them to minister to us. Remember they are also our companion and comfort. In one of those days, I had a misunderstanding with an in-law and I was fuming fire and brimstone in my sitting room, my seven years old son coming in hearing my ranting said "mommy revenge not, vengeance is mine said the Lord". Immediately my emotion felt like a hot rod that just got thrown into a bucket of ice water. I remember in my early days one of my daughters will always correct me whenever I said negative things; it took me time to learn to avoid such. Honestly, she mentored me greatly in the use of words to the positive and it worked out so well for us. We must learn to listen to them and say the positive things always to oneself and the children especially when the worst situations are magnifying themselves. The immediate effect of positive confession is that it gives hope; which is actually the strength we need to move and with that Satan gets disappointed and in anger backs off. God in his own adds frustration more to his anger by manifesting those words.

I don't aspire to be a pastor, but will always love, profess and preach Him in my story. A Widow's life is an embodiment of testimonies of God's grace. So when I say to you to seek God and not man I know what a relief it gives. When you seek and find God's place first in widowhood your peace begins; in that comes all his kingdom glory (Matt 6: 33) that covers the entire gory in hood. His love supplies his abundance even in lack as the Alpha and Omega of all things. Remember He ended that road and started this journey of widowhood and sure will finish it in his likeness. He sees the pain and will seal it in pleasure, just believe he will and work to it. While you continue to believe that God can do it in all situations, look out also for other widows around to share your experiences without shame. She is going to understand. Do not be ashamed. Reject pride and greed so that you don't draw yourself to self-pity. Do not spend time and energy in judging or condemning self even when the world is doing so to you. You errors are common to most and similar to others. Believe in yourself. God has the power to forgive, heal and deliver us tribulations and pain. In prayer and practice strive daily to be a stronger and better person of you not others. Life is a one day at a time journey, so be sure to give each day work your best. Believing on what God has promised not what man has.

Placing one life in God alone will give you a lesser pain in the disappointments of life. Do not let the worry and fear of tomorrow destroy your peace and energy for today. Pray for tomorrow and prepare in today. When you take it each day your burdens are lightened, with the fear reduced. One of the greatest problems of a widow can be the fear of tomorrow, thinking of all the things that have to be done including the dreams we wanted fulfilled. This can really make the pain greater as the fear of most the obvious inabilities are magnified. The burden truly became lighter when I learnt to do what needed to be done for the day, as I left the worries about my tomorrow to God in faith; knowing that he will bring it with good tidings for me as I sing my favorite song then (One day at a time, Christy Lane). There's the power of God that is within each of us to use to push self and pull others. Use it to work and preach your success, share your failures, and dance for your victories. In our preaching the successes be sure to add the behind the scenes, it is what the widow seeks to learn. The rainbow in its colors is visible but the storm isn't. The storm in it that you survived that's the hope in the impossible she needs to hear. It is knowing that she can do it. It is in sharing our failures she is encouraged with the strength to rise and move on. Do you know that in your dancing to victory, the veil in the Hood is not only destroyed but she's moved to look forward to her tomorrow? Yes in it all, the goodness of God is glorified.

SHINE IN GOD

What you believe and say constantly in life has a way of repositioning your state. Wearing of our sorrows as dress and make up in our going out and coming in will drive away motivators only to draw more people that will enhance one's depression. It is better to be alone as widow with your children and work than to be surrounded with unhappy negative people. But be sure you will work harder than usual because even the presence of God cannot exist in a lonely soul. In life's race, people seeing the joy on one's face has rays of hope that is welcoming. When you wear a cheerful smile, your face is magnetic as it conceals the problems and welcomes more smiling faces but with the world on your shoulder it closes you off in appearance and attitude to other. After all no one willingly welcomes a problem. We must learn in handling our problems to do it in confidence with God and whoever he has brought to our path, not in grumbling or lamentations to the public in expectation of sympathy. In whatsoever that is happening, be confident to win. In distress, work hard not to wear it on if you want companies after all it is only winners you know that have many friends. But still be sure forget the size of your friends focus on the size of your dreams. If your friends are more than your dreams the veil of widowhood will be torn instead of unveil. Your friends and family must alienate from you because they will see you as a problem. So showcasing it on your appearance will not only draw them farther away but will block new ones. But in giving it to God in privacy and wearing His joy in public, you will not only keep your friends but will get new ones.

As you collect all the disgrace and discouragement, connect it also into the grace of God. Learn to fly your faith in God to the highest with your words and will. Even as a victim, watch your victory build a theatre that the world will move in to watch its movie in appreciation with you to His glory. To shine in the darkness of widowhood, you must learn to manage the act of discouragement and that of disgrace. An act of discouragement will keep the pride for you to fight the shame but that of disgrace often will strip it off as the shame overwhelms you in pain. As a woman, once you become a widow and you are good looking, if you allow people and their insinuations to get at you, you will almost wish that you are "ugly" though there's nothing of God's creations that is not beautiful. Yet, even at that, the race will still not be easier. With a good look you are automatically alienated from your female friends as they see your "sexuality" as a threat. I withdrew from church societies as I realized women's attitude change once they realize I am a widow. On the part of men Lord have mercy; to most of them you stop having "brain and ability" but only "your womanhood and its activity". To them, the only tool God left with a widow for survival when he took her husband is in between your legs.

If one is to write the experiences of the Hood, what has been seen and heard; it will be a life encyclopedia because it's an unending experience with attending temperature changes. Most widows are bent on saving our children from the pain of knowing all and what their mother went through to keep them out of seeming deficiency in her defect, so as not to overwhelm their lives with pain and bitterness. A young widow with children, in her quest for survival will be seen to spiral out of the wheel in her search of economic freedom and as such she will be exposed to untold viral circumstances. What helps every widow to the glory of God is that as the children grow and the quest for their survival reduces, you automatically streamline the search so as to curtail the abuses received. I remember my daughter asking me years ago "mommy how come you don't go looking for business anymore as before" and I answered her 'I do not need it that bad anymore and as such have to curtail most of the insults I get in the process". The race is sure difficult and the associated disgrace you may get is such that without faith you may turn to a bitter person resulting from anger. But for God, the pain would have swallowed me in shame. Do you know that most women die directly or indirectly because of the things they pass through as a widow as a result of the ripple effect of the pain, the struggle and the anger? The pain has the ability to make one develop illnesses that can lead to untimely death if not managed. This is why we must learn to build our hope in God more than in man. It is only in our faith to the fulfillment of His Word can we walk through all the sinking ground of its exclusion without accumulating the agony. Don't let anyone or anything help or use you to destroy your life. In all your trials; God is not blind. He is more than able to pull one out. He will pull of any deep valley to the highest mountain in victory. We just need to begin and forgive our past.

Do you know in this journey, if you want to write in the world encyclopedia as a widow and you ask for a pen the best you will be given by a few is a pencil, as most will give you nothing while pushing you away. To this what do you do? Will you just be angry and wallow in despondency? No! You can in anger use the pencil, knowing it has it's opportunities of empowering the weakest person to improve with the grace to erase till you get it right. But you can throw away their pencil as I did. You can also use your fingers instead. I, in deciding to write with my finger I lifted my hand to God in tears as I asked for his mercy. I took a leap of faith in the "audacity of His truth" that made clearer these his promises as I experienced in mercy His strength and did the seemingly impossible all at his time. (2nd Cor.12:9, Phil 4:13, Matt 19:26, Ecc. 9:11, Rom 9:16). God took my withering fingers and held it firm as I write to rewrite until, an indelible statement was made from Him for all to learn the glory in His steadfastness. To be widowed and wounded can be beyond one's control but to be whole is entirely our choice. One must work to show that despite the situation, we are better than it seems and will remain so in God with a smile always. Let Him carry you through the height of that mountain. It is achievable. Surrender the pains and fears to God and work your own. We must let go to get whole. This means working at our every opportunity and not just praying at every church program. He will perfect the seemingly impossibilities to our greatness through the small possibility of each opportunity as we become a mentor after the process. Having newly widowed young women share their experience on how other widows had help them in recovery has always been an assessment process for me and this extract from Blessing best summaries the power of mentoring.

She said 'to be a mentor is to be a wounded warrior whose scar has turned into wisdom that witnesses hope to others. In your painful yesterday you've become refined today which enables you to shine wholeness for a tomorrow. Asking young widows how our network has affected their journey. Blessing said, "When my husband died, uncountable questions ran through my mind; where do I go from here? Where do I start from? Who do I run to? A month later I picked up my phone and started surfing on the net for someone who has been in the journey for long, someone who has faced and are still facing challenges; has conquered and still conquering, someone who is ready to tell me exactly what awaits me and how to scale through. Then, Lord connected me to Almanah Hope on Facebook. My healing started the very day I met her, hearing her story changed my life. When we first met, her first statement to me was "my dear you are not the first and you won't be the last. How old are you? She asked of my age and I replied, 30years old. Then she said, "I was 27years then, so you see you are not the youngest to experience it". She made me realize that I can be successful as a widow; her words starred up something in me that kept me awake all night reading her "A widow's window" book. After reading that book, I said to myself; suicide is not the way, Failure is not an option, crying is not the solution, worries won't change a thing and un-forgiveness is too heavy. It is only in Jesus I can find the way, prayer is the key, hard-work is the path, and persistent is the code. Through her I have been able to meet other widows who have done tremendously well for themselves and this motivates my day. *A widow without a mentor is like a sheep without a shepherd which is vulnerable to predators"*.

CHAPTER NINE
FAULTED IN FLAW

Despite your failures and people's judgments about you, don't let your fallen flesh keep you away from the Lord's presence for it is only at his feet can you find absolute love and mercy. And don't be deceived by the glamour of her smiles as a well-made one. As TD Jakes said in one of his sermons "before you can judge my breakthrough, look at my "been through". As a widow, there's no one who can boast of doing it best or have done it perfectly well by her power. Yes, she faulted, so have I faltered. Yet, you need not be quick to judge, you can never be sure what you will do if you are in that vulnerable circumstance. Imagine being faced with the bills and the hunger you see daily on the children's faces as their eyes gleam into yours, it is sure scary; isn't it? This helplessness when faced in those situations takes only God's abundant grace to overcome. The race is not for the strong but for the graced. Yet, be aware as TD Jakes still said "grace looks differently in each person". That beautiful appearance she is wearing has been muddled with all the dirt of the hood and it truly has not ceased. The only thing that has stopped is in the way she wears it. I have learnt with time to take the glory that's in life itself to replace whatever gruesome situation I encounter by being happy with who I am. To me, God's mercy has said 'No' our destruction hence the life and 'Yes' to our decoration hence the everyday opportunity.

My husband's death is an 'end' a destruction to a plan but our life has the begin-again walled with decorations we must work to walk into. Whatever you believe that, will you declare and what you declare is always what will drive your desire. So stop the lamentations and regret, leave the "would-have-been" and make it right with what it is. Stand and start the engine back to the ride at each fall. One of my actions been my strength which I found by agreeing that I do not earned their corset. It wasn't that His grace eluded my place, but that there is a message to which I must learn and the power to master and own it all is still within me. In that I learnt I must walk each path in dexterity to a place of new joy; not only in belief. Every path of this journey is a bumpy one, there's going to be frequent fall at the shortest interval even in your firm stand. I know it because I have travelled through it. You will try in your Will to stand, but yet fall. I can't count how many times I fell, yet rising again to begin, each time I decided to run yet I faulted. This I continued until I learned to stand and walk in God's grace. This brings not just the battle of self to an end but the power to work in grace in the walkway of trials, alerting to begin afresh at each end. When you fight in your power to escape the flaws in the widowhood, when faulted, in the magnitude of shame you remain faltering as the world robs you further with the clays of shame. No one is flawless; don't ever think that your failure is peculiar. When Ngozi affair came out and in brokenness she confided in her pastor after being humiliated before the committee and told him the truth of how she has truly fallen in love with the man, I pastor slapped. She carried the shame for months unable to share with no one until our path crossed.

Though some overcame, most did not but similar is in our experience as each has a failure peculiar to her I said to her. Thank you ma, you do not know how talking you yesterday helped my life she said the next morning. I slept last night. I can't remember sleeping this past three months, as shame and pain have been a great burden on me. My dear, at each end of one's grace hangs another's and the assessment of them are equal to the teacher that owes the course. Your failure isn't lack of God but that of weakness, all we must do is to stand with God not the man of God even in the fall. When you feel dejected or undeserving of His care, it is self-condemnation. Let the society condemn you but never do it to yourself; give it to God in prayer; He can forgive all but you must forgive self. Just strive for godliness more than for perfection, let the self-acclaim perfect people be. Just work to walk in God the only perfect one. Aim daily to be best of you before and in that you get your best each day.

I have to thank God for one of my Pastors in those days who made me to realize that I am not rotten. Unfortunately, some people including Pastors are capable of preaching you to condemnation making you run away even from God in shame. I remember one of those days in my state of flaw, faltered as I felt in my dejection; I went to church truly looking for His grace. I cannot remember the topic of the sermon of that day but what came for me was when he said "if you say you are a born again Christian spirit filled, Holy Ghost baptized that as a man if most beautiful girl stands naked alone in a room with you, you will not be moved. I tell you as a medical doctor go and see your doctor. The Bible said, flee from temptation". He taught me that day that no one is perfect, so I should not be ashamed but rather what I should do is to continuously run from temptations and the likes of it. Simple as it sounds, yet difficult it can be especially as a widow when almost your simplest approach to survival can place you in a corner too enclosed to run as your Will withers.

Dear widow, most of us know what it is to feel ashamed when failed. We are not colored with winning because we did not fall but with the mercy. And remember the joy in all our failed feelings is that it shows that the consciousness of God still exist to help us save the soul. Try, instead of living in that regretful feeling of un-forgiveness that will worsen your situation, to stand on his grace and walk to repentance in humility. It will certainly get better once you keep yourself before the grace of God constantly, gradually and steadily your strength increases as the sins in you reduces till you even seek but won't want it. Our prayers should be for His strength in our weakness; saying always in all circumstances, I will certainly get there, in my lifetime. So, that like Paul, we too can say at last in all 'I have ran and won the race (2 Tim 4:7).

And to you that's quick to form opinion, judge and condemned her not because that is what you get when you do so (Luke 6:37). You can never understand or appreciate her situation, the power of these four in one individual at all times; the fear, pain, shame and grief wrapped around in that loneliness with no intimate confidant can weaken any soul. Weakness, the tiniest ant that sits silence, yet powerful. To me is like an acid that can destroy all natural inhibition of any human being because with the Will wilted; the passion in you power is destroyed. The two greatest forces in life to contend with are that of economic and emotional deprivation. To a widow the quest to confront or overcome her financial hardship and loneliness can be challenging. In one's desperate need for the children's provision, he leaves me with one option of help; in fear and hopelessness I took his option in disgust. Yes, you might say it is not enough reason. For sure that also she told herself; the difference between perception and reality is the need. So in weakness of the situation the need come working strongly against her Will. The reality that is that she is not rejoicing in it, though you think that she took the easy way but that is the hardest of all a women in widowhood will ever have to do to survive in the journey. Most widows never goes for a drop on the palm assistance, they go with a skill to purchase their economy only to see that they're most time required to pay with their dignity to produce the sweat. The most difficult source of livelihood is not to till in strength; it is the tilling in sweat and dignity. The journey sure isn't easy in any way because even in the depression of my lonely state I faulted with a Will. It is mostly a feeling often aggravated. As long as you are in this race to win when you miss your step and have fallen, get up and move on. The position of self-pity or seek pity is destructive.

The act of suffering in Self-denial and loneliness remains a constant battle a widow must learn to contend. Most pretend to have conquered it, especially to the public because that's the drum that's beaten by our culture and religion, but the battle of libido is real. Every soul, spirit and body has its desires. It is created by God and exists in all. It is a feeling which we all move often into, mostly the younger ones. As you daily fight to fulfill the desires of our soul and spirit with the Word of God bombarded to you at all time, the body in its deprivation most often revolts. In prayer, one must strive hard to sustain it but when you fall get up, shake it up, and do not dwell in its shame. What it does, is to immediately get you away from God's presence, which is the sole aim of the devil so that he can then build his own altar of destruction. God is looking out for us not through the windows but through his mercies even in that season. That is why as a young widow remarriage is the best option for a less guilt and fruitful holier life; after all it is till death do us part. When Adam and Eve ate the forbidden fruit in the Garden of Eden, they became ashamed and wanted to hide from God. God had to call them out and told them of their sin which I believed they prayed for forgiveness. If God had left them in their hiding our season of grace would not have been born. Imagine our world without grace, only the mercy of man. It would have been scary! Let's avail of that grace in all seasons. In Him, we do not only find salvation but remain saved with everyday ability to fight temptation.

I tell you, it's actually through grace that, we can after crying and praying in loneliness of the night for the day to break, barely sleeping do we get up the next day to its brightness. In faith we are dressed with a cheerful smile hopeful to grow as we glow, which makes most people want to add to our pain believing all is well as others glorify God in thanksgiving for your victory so far. In the journey through widowhood, the path is a dark, lonely, busy and unpredictable road to ride on. It is not a walkway. You will be forced at intervals to either pulse or run. The distance seem never be completed, as each stage presents a new journey. The road as life itself ends at death, though the trials in time reduces. In each walk, I yearn to be flawless, but fumble within as I walk into a fault unprepared. To each woman you know in widowhood do walk with her in empathy, away from condemnation for her flaws but in compassion seek to hide away to help her weakness. With understanding and support, your cheer can encourage her to build whatever she has lost as she grows back her glow to go on. Her prayers summed up is, "Empathy not sympathy, support not provision".

As a widow, his death opens wide one's world, in wailing God compassionately moves into your home, pointing at every direction to comfort. With the loss of social status, marginalization and reduced economy, all God is asking of us is a recognition of His presence. When we give Him a warm welcome and surrender our worries to Him; He takes over and fight not just our battle but fills the gap so that in each fall He places a cushion to soften the shame that relieve its pain. The beauty of it is that He did not go judging or blaming us but is there to save and bless. The best way of being encouraged is to believe in God's mercy. No matter where you are or have been, once you establish a covenant relationship with Him, day by day you will improve. Life with God and in God is not automatic, let no man or preaching confuse you to shame. You are going to desecrate that altar every now and then if you walk on law or sight. Always remember, some are strong as most are weak, and a continuous gaze on the weak can produce a hopeless perception so also an assessment from the strong. Just focus on God, don't run away nor let the smear destroy your faith in Him. Even in the Bible, abound are people that desecrated the temple of God, but the most important thing is having a genuine repentant heart, working in faith daily to overcome by a palm off all that facilitates the flaws. From experience, I discovered that dwelling in shame and regret keep you feeling worthless and ashamed, placing you away from God and making you less productive as the weight of guilt slows down all your activities. It leads to self-condemnation which can be a self-destructive path that plunges one deeper into the dungeon of the devil.

But learning to go to God in prayer as David did redeems one soonest as you continue the walk as a worthy member of women with grace, whole even when wounded. The joy of redemption is the hope that it brings which keeps one closer each day to the goal. That daily experience leaves one lighter and stronger with better spirit that is not just a great source of strength and hope but a great mentor. The story of David in the Bible was that of weakness of flesh and willingness of spirit. He's called a man after God's heart; I believe he earned that by his constant presence with God in all states, making supplications in prayer with a redeemed heart as he continues in praises and thanks but we must know it is your relation with Him not the church. In the weakness of the flesh he faulted but with his heart constant in atonement with God he rises immediately. He never dwelt in it, never ashamed to the point of shying away but runs back to God, no matter how he has been. That must have been what God saw, the genuine longing heart of man that loves God, wanting always to do his will but falling helplessly most times to his flesh. If David couldn't stand constantly without falling why beat oneself as hard as to shamefully alienating yourself from the very presence of your strength, the creator; who knows our end at the beginning. He has the reality of our strength in His palm and our weakness in His heart. Widowed, and wounded? Learn forgiveness to live whole.

REVENGE NOT

The pain of bereavement and the ensuing treatments are such that must turn a woman into a warrior, but engage the battle in "war room" not in the workroom. It starts with this anger, to him, to God and to self. Day one there were many "if, why and how" but I had to pause to ask myself one day; *"Hope, how can you fight God for taking your husband who is His own or man for killing him, who told you"?* That brought a turnaround perspective as I found out that if I should confront or challenge all actions of life, when will I have the time to be peaceful so as to be productive and happy? Happiness is a choice that should be dependent on one's own decision with actions. God promised to fight all our battles so that we can hold our peace (Ex.14:14), meaning life is a battlefield with peace floating all round. What we choose is what we will get. It means in the thorns are roses but what one hold determines how we feel. How can one choose revenge, since God has decided to do so as against talking the peace he has given us instead? You must not take it upon yourself to avenge. "But madam, my in-laws has taken over so many things that I sweated with my husband said Tessy, over my dead body will I allow them to do so". Are you serious?

Unfortunately she is dead serious. Many women in the death of their husband has lost their asset and with an oppressive culture, a corrupt society and the legal system; you will likely lose your life which many widows has. Let's use the energy and time on issues that concerns your healing and happiness. Vengeance is mine says the Lord (Rom. 12:19). Why fight to take back a battle that has been collected from you at the onset. For all that have been done to you, I know it and I share the pain, it invokes this excruciating passion to fight but don't fight nor allow that evokes the spirit of anger which vomits this bitterness that can lead to un-forgiveness, if you allow it. The load of the hood is more than what one can carry. Take your kids and your life and begin again. It is a big load of work, why add the ABU Virus (Anger, Bitterness and Un-forgiveness) to it? In the CORSET of the hood, you can be stringed to the point of retaliation, with that tiny air left in you just seek peace within and without; otherwise you will strengthen the cord of their corsets tighter to your destruction. My church Pastor, a medical doctor, some years ago listed several physical illnesses associated with un-forgiveness ranging from depression, ulcer, hypertension and many others apart from its power to hindering answers to our prayers. How can one use her hand in blocking her blessings? Or why should one help in destroying one's life when she could choose a fruitful path?

As a widow, when your friends are cold and you are estranged, don't hold it against them, show your empathy too. They are also battling with their own flaws, even the men. A good male friend told me some time ago that why he is very distant is because he does not want to abuse my situation and the friendship. It is truly not all about us. To any friend doing so, I respect and understand their plight and will never hold it against them. Most good friendship that would have been beneficial to widows has been lost because we allow ego to set in. If you have failed to conquer her body, in grudge and hold back your support to her family, what's your place of justification in your assessment of her life? Just because you didn't have it your way doesn't mean she must be so. Nothing in her died with his death, some went comatose but most were resuscitated in time. Her rights to all life offer is still on and with them she's doing the best she can in all earnest.

We are forever grateful to God for being the complete friend; irrespective of one's state. He never peeps through her window, because he is right in the house. He is seeing through the weaknesses and failures. As your friend list reduced or disappeared and fingers point to our failures, he's a friend that will introduce you to new friends whom you will find more helpful. Just open your door to love as the world shut theirs against you. God has the provisions to all that we need, including new friends and a new love. Whatever they have done to you, because we want God's forgiveness of our sins; we must learn to forgive too. Do not hold any of their acts of pain to heart in anger. It is suffocating, injurious and will drown one's joy and peace. Learn to smile more than you can, loosen up and let it go; it is absolutely liberating. Find a reason to understand, the greatest reason you should use is that of their ignorance of your place in God's heart and its benefit to your wholeness. Our responsibility is too much of a burden already, so replace their pain with a plan to live whole. Holding the pain in anger is to be wounded by oneself, you've been wounded enough, heal yourself. Just find in the promise of God greater reasons to let go if we want to be alive and healthy to raise our kids and reap their fruits. To live without anger, bitterness and un-forgiveness is to be widowed, wounded and whole. Let us not cultivate for another to harvest (Isa. 65:22) with this self-inflicted virus. With the physical and spiritual illnesses associated with 'ABU', why will you allow anyone to put you in that state when you can walk away and be free? You will agree with me that a "widow saddled with the untold responsibilities and difficulties associated with raising kids alone cannot afford to add any or all of these sickness because with it you either fail in completing the journey or you succumb at the end of its accomplishments without receiving the crown. Do not allow that to be your portion. Strangle the hate with love which you can see coming from God in your daily victory.

The ABU virus can make one spend not only time, energy and resources on self-inflicted illness but suffer disappointments as a result of unanswered prayers with most things not working as desired. The effect may result either in inability to raise the children as desired, an untimely death or after suffering and succeeding through pains and sorrows with accomplished children to enjoy; sicknesses and pains caused by the virus will deny one of that joy of harvest as death takes over; only for one place to be taken by another person who possibly might have contributed directly or indirectly to the demise. Yes, I can hear you saying God forbid! But determine today to live in forgiveness and leave the revenge to God. It is not easy but it is possible, once you decide to do it. But hey, I have forgiven my in-laws but I just don't want anything to do with them talk less of them and my children said Joy. Well, Joy they are their nephews and nieces. You can say you've forgiven and not allow them access to them. It's painful, but for your peace and joy; even though you claim to have them but the strand of vein I see on you says differently as the emotion is still better, I told her.

This can be a very difficult place to be. At his death, they stole your property and your love. A family you've known for years just one day turns you to a totally stranger with your children. Nothing can be used to explain the feeling. The absolute loneliness is destructive and one day they come back. Just when you've gotten over time and good with your life to seek for forgiveness. You can't forgive them and not have a relationship with them. The simple meaning of family is love and relationship. Forgive and begin again. After all, if God can forgive us, we need to forgive; isn't that what we pray 'forgive us our sins, as we forgive those who sin against us' (Luke 11; 4). Un-forgiveness is destructive; it is a silent killer that we must watch out. It is a very subtle sin, like a leech it creeps in latching on as it sucks one of all glories. I see widows in their bid to flaunt holiness and deeper love for their late husband, brag that they've not and will never have any sexual relationship with any other man, making others feel ashamed, unworthy and condemned. To me, the only less worry of the sins of fornication and adultery, is that one is immediately informed with no justification but to move to agree and accept one sin in guilt and work on to repentance in prayers and supplication. Thank God for Jesus in his action in the story of the woman caught in adultery. The righteous people wanted to stone her, but Jesus Christ saved her by pointing to her accusers that they are equally sinners. (John 8;4;). If Jesus didn't do so, the story would have recorded her death because a whole lot of people would have justified themselves by showing the smallness of their sin to the grievous adultery.

One sin we must beware of in widowhood is that of anger, bitterness and un-forgiveness. Our expectations may never be realized from families, friends and brethren as their treatment are often destructive. This automatically becomes a seed plant of anger that germinates in time, the tree of bitterness; at its maturity it produces the fruit of un-forgiveness. To some people like my friend Joy they do not even know that the tree has grown to suffocate them. That's why I say adultery/fornication remains the least worry because it deals with one to move immediately into prayer but anger, bitterness and un-forgiveness are more dangerous; they creep in subtly and sits on. Those little foxes of envy and jealousy you need to watch as those little words as we say them, "can you imagine him, he used to be in my house 24/7, my husband did this and that for them, she virtually ate out of my pot" etc. You must learn to forget and let it go because most, if not all of those feelings are no longer seedlings but grown tree with ripe fruits, unless you choose to lie to self but not to God. He knows each of that statement brings a feeling of dissatisfaction with a borderline sitting on hate side while looking at love with unloving eyes.

Some treatments seem beyond pardon I tell, but your peace, your joy and your happiness makes it worthwhile. It is worth sacrificing everything not just one thing. When I stopped counting my tales of sorrow and started counting His love that helped me in making perfect that song that says "smile even though you are hurting". It gives that peace which the bible said that surpasses all human understanding (Phil.4:7). With that perception, I can cry to all pain without anger as the soul eject all bitterness making every offence disappear with each closing day to wake truly to the beauty of a new day with hope. God's happiness is best is on our side, always try to replace that trio feeling once it springs up with joyous experiences and expectations no matter how little it seems or how large the harshness of the obvious. It is a very possible experience, though not easy but the ease is worth the chase. Once you desire God can help you make it possible in no time. This truly helps you move to the state of compassion more by excusing every act of unpleasantness as lack of understanding on the part of the person; making it easy to forgive all things and be free from the bondage of the trio Anger, Bitterness and Un-forgiveness. Do you know that the person(s) that put you in that state can either be an agent to deny you of your blessings or might truly be ignorant of his or her actions and as such are happy in their life having fun, while you impede your own happiness?

And to those planting the seed of anger, have you forgotten those warnings? He has promised a severe punishment to such. Widows never lobbied for that, he took it upon himself to do so because of his love upon them knowing what will happen prior to time in their loss with all our feelings and our incapability. God's vengeance is real, help a next widowed get whole and not wounded.

CHAPTER TEN
MY ONE AND ONLY ONE

Many years ago, I said to a friend jokingly when she lost her husband that I do not want to share my husband (God). I almost wanted to monopolize Him, as I made Him become mine. The truth is, you need not worry; as a widow you can personalize or monopolize Him, He is the God of infinite. The 'I AM' is anything you can think of to everyone. So in your path of recovery are tears that will continue to flow. But be sure that at each drop God's towel is dry and wipe enough to absorb it.

A Widow's Tears

Tears, are her process of Tearing Emotions Against Raging Soul. At his death, a widow's emotion is in turmoil, her raging soul looking for a release as she suffocates with the intense pain, the eyes which is the transmitter of her past, the present bringing the future opens up as the boiling steam of her emotions being to flow out. The funny that about the tears of widows is that they are unending, it starts at his death even without the water dripping down the cheek it's flowing within. The dryness of her physical eyes is a confirmation of her bleeding and the travail of the journey is such that even her beauty is designed by tears and travels through the journey daily even to her days of decoration. There are three kinds of tears that her eyes flows often.

The Tears of Anguish

This comes with his death that is her loss. The undignified treatment and actions received, the hurdles to jump and the difficulties of each jump. The blockages to her survival, the disappointments, abuses and injustices received from culture and people. It is the totality of every unimaginable deed received by a widow to which her inability to explain why at each path, can't help but flow out the pains of her raging emotions in tears. Yes, they flow the abundance but they can be converted to joy through God or be a covert of pain and despair.

The Tears of Loneliness

This is the lone tear, always there at every turn mostly in the quietness of the soul manifesting publicly in her privacy; her soul and body dying for a communion often flows out in tears. Even in abundance, the emptiness of her state steers a memory that often time draws the tears. In pain she wails in prayer as the Holy Spirit who in his comfort deep within, robs the balm of Gilead that soothes, heals and dries the tears; restoring hope alive. In joy she comes out to continue her struggle, giving the body a fill of the moment.

The Tears of Joy

Yes, even in the celebration, with all the joys there are tears. It starts from drops to flowing happiness, through the joyful state, yet painful in tale. In the midst of that joy is the disappointment of not having him to rejoice with. In celebrating that victory of success through God's goodness, comes the sadness of the "how I wish". It's the pain of the journey of two that ended in one. It is always a mixed emotion of sadness and joy. It is only God that can help truly wipe away the tears by placing a smile that is deep and beautiful enough to conceal the scars as he continues his job in keeping to his promise of being her protector and provider. As one learns to grow within that all things come from God, it becomes a belief that shields in time all pain especially when the memory of the past walks into the present to corrupt the joy of the moment. God gives and he takes, He alone knows the 'why' becomes our belief.

Godhood in Widowhood

Tessy shared what she experienced from a male friend who promised to assist her pay her house rent when her husband died but asked for sex in return. The man she said, reneged on that promise when she refused to offer herself to him, leaving her helpless. "I thank God because after crying to God to make a way for me, my rent was cancelled by my landlord surprisingly to me" she stated. That's the beauty in the hood. I call it 'Godhood in widowhood'. In all things and situations, you'll experience God anew. He appears in a never known dimension. He has a wonderful way of strengthening one faith in him more in life trials. I think the greatest beauty of life is that of God's glory upon widows. It is really a beauty to behold, totally incomprehensible. Our story remains at all times either a mystery, a fiction or an exaggeration to most people as only very few are able to relate with it. Are you widowed and downcast? Ask God to re-clothe you with his hood to make your life a puzzle of wonders for all to continue to put together.

Get up, get out and get going, stop waiting on who be the 'who' of your dream. Your ability is of God who has allowed it to happen to fulfill the promises of the father of the fatherless and husband of the widow. Reminding God of His promises is the gateway, and the only way to arm one with these promises is to be in His presence, and that is building a relationship with him not with the pastor or the church. As a practice acquired from my parents, going to church activities and programs was a hidden part of my life, no wonder the bible said train up your children the way they should go and when they grow they will not depart from it (Pro. 22:6). I learnt that God is the only way to happy living from childhood. So in my trials I faced Him. No matter the state of things, be sure to have God in your diary. As a practice, no matter how tired, I had three days a week appointment that I had to keep with my children with God. Don't be deceived, there are days I stayed there with no strength and spirit for the Word. But because of the children, knowing I can't do it alone; I was always there. It was a relationship with God not my church or pastor. I never got involve with any society though not discouraging any to but my attention was on him through programs my spirit has welcomed as I finish the rest in my bedroom; my war room.

My constant prayer line were "God these children are yours and you must train them" as promised and peace will be their portion as they make nation. (Isa 54:12). I wanted so much for his signs and wonders to follow them (Isa 8:18) because I knew it was the only way to restore my sanity and dignity that I seem to have lost in loss. The reproach of the widowhood can best be removed by God and the best way of doing so is to help train up our children. It is only possible if we invite and allow him to do it. I had so many phobias but the biggest that hunted most was "Gelotophobia" fear of being laughed at if my children don't turn out right. The advantage of that fear is that it kept me going to God's presence with them even when I do not feel like it. In this hood let rationality and reasoning supersede your feeling, they so many things I felt doing but couldn't and more many I did feel but had to. One of them I had to do no matter how I felt was being in touch with God always with them as I realized that he has the keys to each door of our desire and doubt. I found Him so inside us that we he became our hope. (Col. 1:27). Even when I knew I did not deserve or qualify for his presence, I refused to be away as my soul pants for him

At a time, I became a blackmailer. Yes, but as a blackmailer, the only one I can remember blackmailing and will always do so because it pays me greatly is God. When I realized the bible had every promise to my situation I took my bible study more seriously; though, have never been able to finish the "book of life" but I was fortunate that the Holy Spirit in his mercy guided me to the ones that gave power to my weaknesses and life to end and begin again as needed. In it I got strengthen. My advice, find the Book and see the Words that will take excellent care of you at all times. It is not the church or the man/woman of God, it is His Words in you that provides the comforting feel and a complimenting fill. I remember the first Word I keyed into was that "He is not a man that He should lie, had He said it and not do it?" (Num. 23: 19). Dropping it in my cart, I searched further to find those targeted to victory in my situation. My greatest prayer blackmail when the chips are down and there is nowhere else is "did you not say you are the husband of the widow and the father of the fatherless, that heaven and earth belong to you?" Joyously, l always stand right up without my ability to explain how. Make the Lord your hope, whenever anything is happening pray, work and wait; as his wife and His children, he always takes care. He's not an infidel who cannot take care of his children. How can our kids not have what is their father's? He is God with tides and seasons.

Practice to Principle

Like everything in life, I started this more as an act to practice my faith with a little belief till the results opened up more understanding to the reality of it all. God is truly committed to his Words and widows are top on the list. If one can pause to take a look at those worries, there abound so many other widows whose stories have confirmed to this truth. The power to all provisions is in our hands not in man, though God uses man to supply but we must pull it. God is not just the one need needed by man to receive all needed but the door that opens to that doors that will lighten the seemingly darkness with the ability to lighten our burden of widowhood. Often people don't see the weight of the load you carry because God has taken it off in that smile, as it feels light while looking heavy to others. Give him the weight of the journey and he will give you his ease. (Matt

11:30). This is not just the physical burden, that most times can be easy to deal but the heftiness of the emotion in that loneliness. He alone gives an unconditional comforting relief that comes without guilt. My testimony to my sister widows in this, is to assure you if in any doubt that God is right inside your case, it can look sometimes as if he's not. But he is. All we need to do is to keep moving, at each obstacle, purse but begin immediately.

As a young widow the work is made lighter when God takes over the training of your children. How can you be a father to the children, especially the sons? The man character at a stage of their training becomes imperative, it is only God that is capable of filling all voids in his ways in his provision, I call Him "one and only one' as he positions a guide at each crossroad.

His Sufficiency

No man can lighten the load of emotion not even the 'remarrying' but for God. I believe the vacuum of 'ex-relationship' in widowhood can only be whole through God, if not; it will remain a sore spot even in a new one. A good friend of mine shared a story of his broken marriage to a widow and the issue was that she couldn't get herself to absorb truly with her son into their new family as in everything and every time she felt and sounds a stranger. There is usually the battle of fear. You can destroy every disgrace and discouragement by simply throwing them away into the trash and moving ahead but that load and its yoke will stay if you don't hand it over to God and work hard to be in the present without comparison. It is only in building trust on the future that your ability to overcome grows to suffocate the multitude of fears that will be contending with each possibility. Knowing when your end has become your waterloo, so that you can swim off.

I remember after the most humiliating experience I had in 2007, in between the tears and pain of that day, in consolation I smiled to myself; saying this is it. I must bow out from this kind of business. I have seen, heard and taken a lot in my line of business but that was the rock on the cake not the icing. The grace of God though sufficient for one, we must learn not to stretch it otherwise we abuse it. We should seek the wisdom of discernment, which is always a guard to our actions. The life challenges in widowhood are in dimensions in each stage with non-easier in bearing. At his death to most, especially the young ones while fear of economic survival will keep you occupied in search of opportunities but with the children settling down to their own comes the pains of loneliness. It is at this stage we realize the lack of a companion.

As I stopped my business in 2007 due to my awful experience, I realize that the work has been of great comfort. The lack of activities almost led me to a state of depression. Hi Hope, are free today? Can we gang out at club today for a drink Dele asked me? No! Girl, this is the time you've turned it down and yet you just sit home. Yes I know, I don't know but I just don't have the … throwing out my hands; what do I call it? If not that it is me, I would said I am depressed. What do you mean by "that is you"? Nothing can depress me I said. Well girlfriend said Dele, I have news for you. I have been wanting to say it to you but glad we are here. You are acting depressed, there is no life you since you stopped that your procurement business. Immediately, I got into the bedroom dress up and hey guy, let's go to the club. That night as he dropped me off, it hit me hard that truly my emotion was sick. From 1994 to 2007, I have been superbly business, kids, work, business and interval recreation. I never know or may never had time to feel my emotional sadness till lately. Kids grown, business ended and all my oomph just disappearing in my very eyes. In order to manage my state I had to go back to school while looking out for other things to start to add to my work in prayer.

Weeping may endure for a night but joy cometh in the morning, (Psalm 30:5). I believe it is widows alone that understand the real meaning of that scripture. There are truly days you wake up after the cold lonely tearful night, with all the enthusiasm of life's joy and hope , comparing it with sorrows of the previous night you wonder; what a transformation. To me that is what sufficiency means. It is all about the grace in (2 Cor. 12:9). In our weakness his strength is perfect. So try not carry the weight of the sorrow around, drop it at all times as much as possible as the sun alights to a new day. It is new and bright as the steadfast love of our God. (Lam 3:22-23). Wake up with the faith, yes today is the day; it wasn't for yesterday. In that hope one's expectations of joy have the wheel for breathing life to living that makes everything alive. The danger of grumbling today on yesterday is that it takes life away from today making the day life in jeopardy and as she seeks in sympathy. I strongly refused that widows are made an object of pity or ridicule, but be sure not see or make yourself one either. Wearing the gloomy face will not make anyone help you. It will rather drive them farther away. It is only in God that 'we will' wake up with 'I can' to get out the 'I will' power that are sure tonic of survival.

Prayer is Our Insurance

A widow said something to me one day that I found very deep; she said, "Hope, our prayers to God are like an insurance premium, not used immediately but very useful in all, each day". It can be doubtful, especially when one doesn't get a direct answer to her desire but the truth is that the growth in our life is a manifestation of our words, wishes and works. Often people think prayer is just about the 'kabashing' of tongues or just a religious practice. No! They are the words of our mouth and the meditations of our hearts. They are dreams of our thoughts and the desires of our hearts; those fantasies of our future in the present.

The hope we grow in despair that comes from the sovereign power above. Store up your barn with prayers and thoughts of hopefulness; they leave the earth in faith to heaven to come down in seasons like a flood through the gate of heaven breaking into our life. When the storms of life begin to increase, do not be discouraged. Do not allow people to either to make you lose the dream. Keep your hope alive to that desire, even when the sight to it is blurred, be thankful and find joy in each of journeys; find the "begin" card at each end. I have learnt to find joy in my hood that no one can take away by having a grateful heart to the smallest good of it all. Though it will be nice to ride in private jet but the joy of life is not attached to it, it is found in happiness of contentment. What is happiness to you? The success of life is relative, but the real success to me is in the end to begin, a chance the dead did not have, a great privilege of the living. The fact that I ended the struggle without ending with the day is success and to wake the next is an opportunity to begin again and rewrite the history that I wrote. Happiness in life remains an opportunity to live. Take every downturn in grace of the lesson not in disgrace, whatever its form, whenever it comes but do not let it steal your pride. The place of happiness is found on how you walk through to weather the storm.

One must learn to throw away every life debasement no matter the weight so as to be able to smile away its pain. Make your widow companion prayer; "looking unto Jesus, the author and finisher of our faith." and learn to look up to him indeed, and in need the Lord will surround you with compassionate people. In grace I assure you, you will sing songs of victory as they tell the tales of your success. *A Widow's window* is not only on her face. Though you seek to see a lonely eye but finds a glittering smile, it's still in the concealment of that shine. In all, her tears that flows underneath the skin of her cheeks falls the joy of assurance and comfort. Her HOPE is in the abundance that glows in her smiles. As you continue in this journey learn to be thankful to the tiniest kind of kindness in all seasons, in there lies His love for though we often say to love him, but he loves us most.

If you ever want to understand the journey, the best you can do is to try to look into your eyes in the mirror closing them. What's your image? If you can understand the state of your feeling right there, be sure her state most often present worst of that imagination. Her feelings you see in that smile is a grateful heart though in pain of a great loss stands in full even in her hole to hold on God as she continues to get whole. As her face curves to the smiling lips and her body tweets in yearn, so does her hope hops to the promises of the future refusing the state of the present. Though, often, in situations of fears I still grieve my loss; yet, it's so comforting to find happiness with love. Taking always the full of compassion of a great friend as companion. I though, not too proud of most of my deed, yet the premium I have placed on my heart's meditations has affirmed me that His mercy speaks on me. The rock that stands firm is His goodness and on that we will ride to conquer. Standing on His promises in widowhood has given me the only definition of hope I know; Hope is that tiny light shining out as you are covered in the hood which is strong enough to clear the darkness.

CHAPTER ELEVEN
LONELINESS, THE ABSOLUTE POVERTY IN WIDOWHOOD

A Lonely Walk
In his death culture struck
To change the sound in her name
and stain the purity of her step
As it paints her bricks a color.

With dark poured her path
It separates her wall
In the hallway of world
as walks in identity of shades.

The dignity of her being
Is swallowed in shadow,
Of everyone's imaging
they've tailored on her image.

She's dressed so different
from her world once dreamed
in a way chosen by her kind
Only to rip off a strength once
owned.

Yet, in that hole she tirelessly tiles
To walk back to one she once know
Through the lone walk she seek still
the fame once desired as own.

Alone feel
A lone she wails in flavor,
the aroma of her past
As the sight of each day,
drowns the soul in her desire.

Yet, the shade of next night
enlarges the hunger of her lack
Aloud her body screams
As it spells in words her night.

The tempest of her body
known best to her bed
To which her soul longs a halt
remains a wound opens to heal.

The sores of it draws the flees
As dogs often falls to lick
bruising most times further the
sore that makes her loss the scar.

As the fullness of her emptiness
Steers a comfort from above
the stillness of her spirit
Witnesses the depth of a love
by the hand so strong in hold
to the yearning of each her a fall.

Alas she end to begin anew her
world
In luxury of her dream to blossom
enclave in memories her loss
to begin yet again to live.

Loneliness is often an intrinsic loss, defined in the extrinsic. It is the emptiness of the inward being, the vague of the feeling within, present one in a state of condition that opens to physical, mental and social illnesses. It creates an unhappy and depressed emotion that often dresses one with a resentful personality; if unchecked. When the lonesome disease is allowed to abide within, if you are not aggrieved to a state of aggression; one can be drowned in the sea of withdrawn. The falling to the worst of the state of one's personality is a manifestation of loneliness. A question I often ask young widows when they take the complete assumption that companionship is not necessary is 'How fun and fulfilled do you think it is for one in sharing the sadness, burying the burden, telling the tale, and enjoying the joy alone'? To most it strikes the right cord of the hole within. As God said in His Word, "It is not good that man should live alone" (Gen. 2:18). In like manner, it is not good that an adult should live alone especially one that tasted the joy and sadness of togetherness. So grateful to the power of Holy Spirit who remains the greatest comforter. But for God, can't help but wonder how many widows would have survived, especially those living in most of my African society where cultural practices and rites has defined them "unclean". Making them seen most as an outcast.

But the reality is that in appreciation of His work we must do our own work. As a widow, while we must first hold on to God; but we should not forget that happiness is a choice taken not given. We should begin to take all actions that will bring happiness to us as we allow God to complete it. The life of single parenting, especially for a widow is a life tied on a string of 'alone', in an 'a lone path' you'll trade to live but don't over burden yourself with its worries. God is there always to grace one with testimonies of abundance for each lack in every activity. My own life in particular has been that of one testimony after another despite the abundance pain and loneliness encountered. So will be yours, just choose to count your blessings more than compiling the sorrows. We must learn to anchor the boat of our life to God, he's the only way to guarantee we remain afloat as the warmth of his breeze in this cold ocean of loneliness blows daily on you.

For so many years said Moji, Christmas was a period I did not look forward to as I always felt without the man in the equation we were not a complete family and so had no business celebrating. As the years passed, I tried going on occasional vacations with the children within the limits of what I could afford but then, the children do have their fun while I returned with not much satisfaction or fulfillment as the adult companionship was missing". In season of festivals and outing, the sight of couples together and its funfair becomes a lonely drama in an opera theatre making it heavier. At that, one would have preferred being at home in one's abode, but for the children who need their fun for total nurturing. It is our duty to raise the children and give them all that is required for total wellbeing irrespective of one's state.

As a widow, one have to learn to function in social outings as it can seem unwelcome especially in adult and family gathering. You learn not to be on the space of any couple so as not to evoke the anger of any woman or the gossip of the gathering, especially a young widow. This usually results in our turning down most invitations. It is advisable when younger with young children, going on Christmas or holiday festival, it is important to find a not too family tied show so you can function better without you and the children standing out. But irrespective of what is going on in the struggle of widowhood, be assured that God will always show up just at the point where you have tried all and it seems like there is nowhere else to go with no one to hold. In all the trials, troubles and weaknesses, his outstretched hand for you to fall into and be comforted is always there.

"There are so many lonely days and nights especially when the children were much younger and more emotionally demanding. They demanded so much attention and in giving it, all my energy was sapped with no one to cling to for support". In the heat of that pain comes the frustration of loneliness, on her bed she clings to the pillows with the Bible in between as tears flows down like a fountain on her pillow. The gratitude in the gravity of widowhood remains that even in that as the kids in their demand creeps to add gasoline in the burning emotion, as you hear that name 'mommy'; the grace pulls again the strength that dries the tears. Like a Sahara it immediately clears to behold the child in love. All their emotions as children are packed on one parent as they choke you with their demand and attention; It is only as a widow that you sometimes wish that your name 'mommy' can go on vacation even for a day, to give you time to know if you still know who you are. Yet, in most of her void, filled with that mood of total exhaustion and lack, dying for love and attention she braces up to welcome the children's need for attention and love, despite the fact that it is the love of a man that you desire most at that time. In the children's need for attention one must learn to give what we lack most; love, affection and attention. Absolutely wonderful.

Loving kids is a big beautiful burden and without him to share it, the emotion can indeed be very weighty. In this state one cannot help but to weep the lonely tears of want and often long the desire of a companionship till you are satisfied for the moment. It is very exhausting. I find most widows in the shame try to deny this as they prove their love for late husband or the extract ordinary power of God in them, don't be ashamed or disappointed of self, just embrace your weakness as it is, but immediately Will up your strength again. Yes, give it to God and get graced with the glory that is indeed sufficient for you. The children remain a great companion, even when they are not at home, they mommy you each second that it gets glued to the memory, playing constantly on replay. They are truly a source of strength to women in widowhood. They do a great job in filling the void, yet they must grow out of the house in their process of evolving into adulthood. This is why I usually frown at the culture and religion, when they downplay the teaching and preaching of remarriage, apart from the sexual need of marriage, is that companion especially at old age.

It's so easy in our society, even a married woman living with her husband to advise a widow when it comes to relationships and remarrying "what are you looking for; stay for your children". If that's all it is for, why then is it that women still remain married to their husband when they are no longer bearing children? When these children are grown up and out on their own, what happens to the widow? The life of a woman in widow is a tricky one.

"Having been widowed for over 17 years said Pauline, with children now mature and grown up; I realize that I have been running my life as a program. I unconsciously developed software that seemed to be working for me in every aspect of my life, the home, career, finances, children and even the unexpected. I have become so independent without my knowing that life just passes me by unnoticed most times". So true, as a young widow, the work of your life and the children remain a full program for you to juggle on within the hours of the day even unto the night and that reduces the level of loneliness as you almost forget who you are. In there the fallacy of the financial "need-only" assumptions in widowhood remains hidden as one struggles through a structured approach to survival forgetting we are a three part being; spirit, soul and body. The spiritual blackmail further empowers one as she works by the illusion that only water runs in her vein as the blood dried up at the burial. With the children grown, the automated program will seem to be corrupted with a virus as most jobs that go with children are gradually deleting presenting an entirely different level of loneliness to which we must learn to adjust again. There's a deeper pedestal of loneliness that occurs when the kids are grown and out of home that if unchecked to me is the reason most widows begin to battle one illness or the other.

The kids must leave home one day; we do understand and appreciate it all. Who can blame the kids or the widow? While in their growing away we must create another life that can help our wholeness, one must also learn to pause and answer most questions that pops up at each bend of the journey. "Most times, I can't help but ask myself; where am I headed and what does the future hold for me in old age" said Moji? These and so many other questions will continue to arise with not much honest answer, I must tell you as society continues in their assumptions to expect from you what they can't give. But we must quickly learn to address it truthfully from within otherwise in time you won't understand if your loss is the loss of husband or the loss of oneself. The biggest disenfranchisement to widows in our Nigerian culture especially most tribes in the South is the dichotomy between culture and religion, the inability of both to take the good of each and acculturate it down to the society remains an abuse that women struggle with in widowhood. Imagine a widow in her 50s who was married for over 20 years before husband passed away, in her advice to a young widow in her early twenties with less than 4 years marriage; who in asking an honest question "how does one handle sexual urge"? Her answer was that she prayed to God to take away the feelings at the burial of the husband and God did.

What an absolute fallacy, and a manipulation of the young lady's emotion. She has totally condemned her making her feel ashamed. But in truth, it's what culture built in and religion plastered it. A woman in her fifties with years of marriage has no same degree of sexual demand as a lady in her twenties with a few years of marriage. Her libido was just blossoming, it's apple on the tree of her life just about to ripe when death struck and as such cannot be weeded out as a thorn that has wrongly grown in the farmland.

The battle of physical, social and emotional wellness is real and is a struggle that continues to keep one as a widow dangling between the right and wrong side of morality and religion as questions abound; but with all, there is one answer. Remarriage an option, very religious; the traditional, Muslim and Christianity welcomed it in their practice. It is Biblical and one should desire, pray and work to it without worries. Just be certain and confident that God's peace is filled with greatness in the future (Jer. 29:11) and go for it. Whatever the desire, all one must know and resign to, is that God is in control. I just cling unto his mercy taking what he brings by day in thanksgiving while seeking. In a widow's life, the day comes with feelings of contradictions, it is fun and loneliness, laughter and quietness, gratitude and worries, appreciations and demand, and it is always that of mixed feelings.

Yet in all, in the loneliness He comforts, in our worries He consoles, in our demands He completes, in our appreciations His compliments, in our laughter His conquest, in our weakness He strengthens and in our failure He works. No matter the words for our emotions, His provision is precedent because of His ever presence. Beneath that beauty lays an emptiness that is characterized by abstract lack that most often send her into search of her physical needs. With all its pains she reaches a point that defines success yet that hole instead of getting filled widens as the depth opens an entirely new feel that cannot fill an atom of space. The lack of understanding of this cycle creates a feeling so difficult to articulate; only the fact that we most often learn late as it becomes clear that loneliness is the absolute poverty in widowhood. Yet, even in that the fullness of His joy in which one can find peace, shines the hope she has built over the years to which others finds the strength to live through on their journey. The lasting comfort of the soul that holds on when over the body is only in the love of its creator who owes it but gave it the body as he becomes that "something inside so strong"; the seed that grows His hood to unveil her hood. His love is the armour to which we are leaning on that shines out in her smile, that not even your thought, path or act can eliminate.

CHAPTER TWELVE
WIDOWS AND CULTURE

Caro said when her husband died in 2012; "I flee from our village at mid-night with the assistance of security personnel. Before I could come back to Lagos after the burial, her in-laws came to our house and packed up everything, leaving only my clothes and my child's own. Then, I had my daughter expecting the second child one. Our landlord on seeing the whole scene play-out, ejected me out of the house. Though I was advised by some people to go to court, I was too broken and weak for more traumas especially with my pregnancy and financial state. In pain and scarcity I moved into an uncompleted building with my child and pregnancy. I started a catering service, cooking and hawking it at the motor parks. My child delivery labour was traumatic and complicated; I was moved from one government hospital to the other as most of the hospitals rejected me". Thanks to the assistance of my Pastor and the mercy of God, I gave birth finally after five days of moving from one hospital to the other in labour. I have managed to move into a bedroom apartment with my two kids; some days are good but most days are worse as I continue in the financial, social and emotional struggle of widowhood with none of my in-laws ever asking after their children."

Most African cultural norms and widowhood are something that need total reorientation. While the cultural practices and rites are said to be reducing, the residual effect remains harmful. The hypocrisy in its abolishment is so shameful. This puts the vulnerable widow in a battle of self, societal perception and assumptions. Every rite practiced does not showcase a loving wife, and the psychological impact of it to the widow, her kids and the society is harmful and unproductive. A young medical student was hit on the street nine months after the father's death, and the explanation given to it just to continue to institute the culture of abuse in widowhood was that she challenged her mom on her acceptance to undergo all the degrading and horrendous experiences such as eating with cellophane bag, shaving hair; the head, pubic and armpit to which they termed it was a challenge to culture; therefore the reason for her death. This is after watching her father terminal illness of cancer for over three years.

What we have refused to accept and address is the mental state of women and her children when in their loss of a loved one; a father and husband, the amount of fear these practices further exposes them to. Widowhood is one of those silent pains in life and there's no way of defining a loving wife from the degree of pain the culture inflicts on her nor will it build bond in the family. Rather it has created a rigid dichotomy in our culture helping to crack the concrete wall of African society of extended family especially the patriarchal system; as children in the death of their father often loses ties with the paternal relations in their refusal to forgive what the uncles and aunts did to their mother and their abandonment.

WIDOWS AND THE CHURCH

While I agree without doubt that widows strength is entirely on God, her support goes beyond spiritual and finances to her physical needs; she has her psychological needs involving her emotional desires. Most of our religious groups especially our churches are in truth not doing enough on this. Though some are more supportive than others, but I believe that churches apart from prayers should have laudable social programs that accommodate the widows. Today, there are all sorts of activities for the single, divorced and married but the (un-divorced married single) that is, the widows are locked in between. This produces a feeling of unwelcome, marginalized, confused and even unhappiness; thereby increasing her state of loneliness. A whole lot of widows have turned to religious prostitutes moving from one church to another in search of this, with most of them not knowing what they are searching for.

Everyone wants a place to fit into, it's about the psychological need. But often, one finds that same feeling of outcast exists in our churches though with a different shade. As Zaram said, "though we were well-known and respected, with my husband, a very prominent contributor to the church activities. After his death I had to change church because of the attitude of most members of the church. The cultural presentation of widows in shame is seen to transcend from outside into church as both the pulpit and pew are careful of not being seen to be supporting or encouraging the widows. Widowhood is real, and as the singles and married exist with their needs so do widows too. The silent state of affairs concerning widows in our churches should be replaced by an average degree of salient activities. Among the human motivational needs that widows struggle to get satisfaction from are 'sense of belonging' and self-esteem. It is about being recognized in our community for who she is without stigmatizing her to which our church is one of the most important.

Building an atmosphere that is capable of creating avenue for 'sense of belonging' is one of the ways widows can be empowered. In churches we hear of couple's dinner and singles night coming up regularly for the couples and the singles accordingly. What about the widow? Where does she belong? Where is her social inclusion? Mentoring program with spiritual and social activities is very important as it creates a better atmosphere for sharing, understanding and supporting each other in an obvious comfortable arena. What most church programs do is to continue to spiritually bombard her in all activities forgetting that in taking up the role of 'husband' as God ambassador; the must also provide recreational activities that are satisfying to her. This helps to build the body better in readiness for more spirituality. My question to men and women of God with others that gather widows always to preach and pray; do you think she hasn't heard enough? Yes, there's never enough Word or prayer but "is prayer the only communication you have with your spouse and loved ones?

Another area church can help empower widows are in preaching not counseling on remarriage. Preaching remarriage of widows is a sermon and teaching that should come from the pulpit so that the congregation who turns to be the society will begin to reorient their mind. It can never be seen or taken to encourage or celebrate widowhood. But in counseling apart from being unproductive to young widows when the society sees her 'unmarriageable' with the church presenting her as "Jesus wife" it leads to ungodly entanglement with men of God. In his stand on young widows, Paul through the inspiration of the Holy Spirit maintained remarrying, (1Tim. 5;14). Paul said, young widows should be encouraged to marry. I am sure if he were here, he will add; by encourage I mean not just counselling her but also preaching it so that she can enjoy both personal encouragement but also encouragement from her society through love, support and acceptance

The biggest challenge in remarriage in our society is the dichotomy of culture and religion. While the Muslims and their culture seems to have an understanding of practice in their transition; the Christian and its culture is yet to, especially in the presentation of its theory and principles. Most of our non-Muslim ethnic groups practice the Christian faith even without being fully acclaimed Christians as they've abandoned the old traditional practices that they perceive to be crude and uncivil. But when it comes to remarriage in widowhood there seems to be a big gap as the church, from the pulpit to pews are caught between 'sacredness and fear' in addressing the issue. The most worrisome is the fear of not being seen to be encouraging wives to go kill their husbands so that they can remarry. Growing up in a culture, where we watch our mothers, fathers and elders saying to widows, "what are you looking for again, stay for your children", then going to church and hearing our Pastors saying 'Jesus is the husband of the widows'; what most widows come to experience later having been indoctrinated with the above is the effect of these on their sexual and emotional well-being.

The worst being the spiritual blackmail that happens in any occasion you are engaged in chatting with members of your church or the Pastor; he or she will say to you that it is Biblical to remarry. This is a societal manipulation as we are torn between culture and religion. The effect of these actions on society is the reason while a young man is psychologically constrained to venture into the idea of marrying her the "widow" even when he finds every other thing right except that "she's a widow". A young man said to me; when I asked himhy he couldn't marry a young woman he found a great chemistry with. Ella said, he is not man enough and Betty said "he is a true child of God". I say he's a product of our culture to which Christianity did not complete his conversion not just on him but his family especially the mother and society who is going to raise the eyebrows and "tongueroll". It can be a hell lot of battle said Francis who married a widow; which he said years down the line war is still on with so many family ties that's untied trying hard to tie back.

I have heard Pastors and Christians discussion on this issue and have developed some school of thoughts among them.
The first school of thought says preaching remarriage is not a pulpit topic but a counseling discussion. My submission to this is, if we continue to counsel a widow and widows that they can remarry; will she or they marry themselves? A young boy who all his life has witnessed from culture saying to a widow stay for your children to hearing openly the next minute that Jesus is the husband of the widow right from his Sunday school days; how does he relate this to seeing a beautiful young girl in life hallway and in friendship that obviously has love with a marriage potential; In his further interaction realizes that she is a widow. Would you blame his pull back reaction? We should also not forget that these young men are not ignorant of both the silent and open discussion of widows killing their husbands' cultural assumptions and assimilation. They are going to have parents especially the "dear mother", his family and the society who are going to have trouble understanding why in the midst of the world population of women and girls, it is a widow he has found suitable to marry. With all these complication that has been magnified by our culture, it is very likely the young man naturally or forcefully will fall out of love or at most, explores the relationship knowing from the onset it will lead to nothing as he finds himself a wife daring to keep the relationship if he's allowed.

The second school of thought says it is not preached because they are being careful, you don't want the husbands to go attacking the wife at the slightest issues "yes you want to kill me so you can remarry after all, the pastors told you so. This set pastors I have tremendous respect for. Pastors are human beings and agree they are cut between the spirit being and human factor. Working to keep the sanctity of the married is worth the effort, but the question is, isn't that of the widows worth saving too; considering the percentage increase that will continue even without the men's accusations and assumptions? After all, we as Christian believe that life and death is in the power of God, he gives and he takes as such whatever we do death is inevitable.

The third school of thought is those that says, if it is the will God it will still happen; these are found among our brothers and sisters in Christ, especially the sisters. I call them hypocrites because they know the fact they hide under the statement the "will of God". I am not trying to be blasphemous, I love, respect and reverence the Trinity, because I am absolutely nothing but for God who has made us in his likeness giving us dominion over everything with mental ability to use every word of His to live daily. So a discussion of widows and remarriage and the role of in preaching it so that the congregation can develop a mental acceptance and what as a Christian you have to say is that "if it the will of God" she will marry. My question is why do send your kids to schools to be taught by the teachers? You could leave them at home and pray for the will of God on them as Engineers and other professionals to materials. I can't help but state this, try to compare the effect of tithe preaching today with what will happen if a very little balance attention is given to preaching widow's remarriage in particular and its issues in general.

The last but not the least school of thought are the "ifs, will ``and what" of the widows themselves; her conspiracy of silence. They are all summed up in her fears, which be highlighted in subsequent pages. Churches should create programs for widows to mentor themselves and not just leave pastors to be the sole comforters of widows to which they can only be through the words. As the Pastors give the word and prayers afar, a mentor presents the facts and needed encouragement in close relationship but without temptations.

It is truly in both, the soothing words of hope that eases emotional burden, and a mentor's practical experiences that her strength and hope is fortified. It will also involve associations, recreations, relaxation and sharing of common experiences. In life everything is in transiting because it goes as one phase is ending, so is it for the day, at the end of it all, a widow goes home alone to her lonely hood. She cannot, at most times call a friend, male or female that is married or even her Pastor at mid night when the demons of loneliness come around and her sleep is taken over by pains and frustration. At such times, even tears are not available to soothe the feeling. But she can when she is too broken to use her prayers, songs and promises of God's word call a mentor to talk or chat with. I had a younger widow calling one late night telling me her true state of absolute helplessness and loneliness, asking me how I have managed all these years. I remember chatting with her in total honesty and by the time we ended about 2.20am of that day, our discussion had drifted to a more joyous event which for sure, have not only oiled her soul but had equally smoothened my state as I too received a healing in the sharing.

WOMEN AND WIDOWS

Women we are said to be our worst enemies, very unpatriotic statement to our world but if you watch what women do to their fellow women in this widowhood race you can't help but agree to the statement. The activity that takes place in our cultural practice is undertaken by women. How can a woman and her children lock her widowed daughter–in–law away with her grandchildren from their home; isn't she supposed to show some understanding. My question has always been who invented these practices in our cultures that deal with widows, was it the men? I suppose so, all in their quest to conquer, subdue and possibly control women. The man remains the head, we believe strongly in their headship authority and love for them to continue to live it and not show it. It is only through understanding and agreement of the strength in weakness of the women that both sexes can maximize their potential in perfect harmony.

But if the men did introduce it, why do women embrace it with absolute joy of purpose? Couldn't we have made it easier for ourselves since we are the executor of the policy? Why do we carry it with so much passion forgetting we may be there someday? Widowhood is in the life cycle of every woman, once you say "I do". It can be terrible what widows have to bear from our fellow women. The activities of widowhood is enforced and monitored by women as the men are never close enough to do so. They observe every action, reporting and comparing notes with one another for approval or condemnation. You find most women look forward to a gathering where they can humiliate the widow for the flaws they will see in her. A widow finds her joy subconsciously controlled by their conditioning. She's often most scared of being joyous for fear of people's interpretation and confrontation. It's easy for women to label widows as they give them names they will never love on themselves.

In other women's assumptions, widows are a constant reminder of sorrow; a feeling that sorts of ask one why rejoice and be glad in the day that the Lord has made. The only reason she excludes herself from celebration, is the rolling eyes of her sisters telling her she should not be there, and that 'beautiful' in her world if not for that man; of whom they can point to any that passes by you with a smile. Most women make sure that indeed the widow lives through the mood of widowhood. At any display of success they are quick to label her as promiscuous. They are often so glad to attach her conquests to the glory of a man with no credit to her in any ability but the sexuality.

The Uphill Task of Remarriage
The challenges in remarriage in widowhood can be enormous, though the fear of it has stolen the fun in it. They come in different forms and from social, religious, personal and emotional angles. Yes, while religion and culture support remarriage, they both offer it in an entirely different way.

The traditional culture of the Levites marriage must have originated from the bible, depending on one's belief because some who practice other religions might say it was there before Christianity. Either way, it is a win-win situation; meaning that it was a practice acceptable by the society of old. Traditionally, when a man dies, the wife is made to choose one of husband brothers, cousins or kindred. Every culture in our society has their process of deciding who in the lineage is qualified. While some widows might have been lucky to willingly or been chosen by one of their choices, others have been known to have forcefully done so. The fact is, like every other things in life, it has its advantages and disadvantages. Even as a Christian it changed the story of Naomi and Ruth to glory. Because it was an acceptable practice, the widows at that time were not shunned, scorned or segregated in the act rather to most of them, it created an emotional, social, spiritual and financial security in its own way.

Today that culture has faded out. The practice is no longer fashionable. Christianity condemns it, as it legalizes adultery and practice of two wives. It is also seen to violate human rights principle especially where widows and men are coerced into accepting it. The act of forcing a widow to an in-law she's not affectionate to or the widow choosing an in-law who she is not attuned to such but must due to cultural demand is a violation of human rights; so it is for the legitimate wives who are coerced to accept the existence of the widowed sister-in-law with sealed mouth as they both share the man. As a fight from that woman is a fight with the culture, as such unacceptable. But as these traditions are fading, the religious culture emerged. It also had a provision for it knowing the importance of the practice that is in living a healthy life. Health, as defined by the World Health Organization (WHO), is "a state of complete physical, mental and social well-being and not merely the absence of disease or infirmity."

Though the argument of its implementation remains but the facts indicated that the three domains of human being; spirit, soul and body should be considered when measuring the health status. While we expect the church and the society to work together to build a road path where young women at his death in time like the widower can pray, seek for love to find her again; and when it does she can respectfully welcome it without being undermined in any form. The widows too must learn to cut the cord of fear to which we've tied out the possibility of a second chance to live in love with a man again.

In a questionnaire to widows on why they haven't remarried and /or the likely obstacles to such decision; below are the summary of our thoughts and words as was written;

Fear of the people's assumptions and perception. What will my mom say? How will his mom feel? What will society say? How do I face them? What will my church say? How will they look at me? Will they think I didn't love my husband well enough?

Fear of having to start again. My new husband's, does he have children, his family and friends; will they accept me? Will he accept my wanting or not wanting more kids? Will I see the kind of man I really desire? Will I be forced to settle for the available? Can I find someone to love me the way my late husband loved me?

Fear of being with another man, who is he? Can he be trusted? Will I be able to love him as I loved my late husband?

Fear of failure. What if that one dies again? What if that man turns a beast? Will he love my kids as his own? Will he molest my children, especially my daughters? How will he treat my kids? Will he take care of my kids with his own without dichotomy

Fear of not knowing how to keep my kids from thinking I'm replacing their father. Fear of being sure my kids and my next Chapter are truly happy.

Fear of being too set in my ways. Where do I start? I have been independent for too long, can I still know how to be a wife?

In reality a high percentage of widows seem to be suffering from Phobophobia (fear of fear) as I found the list of widows challenges to remarriage were unending. But it is obvious that the totality of these fears migrated from our cultural practices and religious upbringing, not downplaying our inherent nurture nature. But the number one obstacle is being locked out in theory and practice by the two dictates of the society in their evolution, with remarriage mostly not expected nor encouraged. A widow's sexual desire is made invisible in all her empowerment discussions. As society shies away from it while she hides under her religion, *she is in most people's eye unfit by 'would have been' her class for relationship and marriage; just because of her status.* In widowhood and remarriage, it is generally the fear of not getting what one really desires that is the calamity of her invisibility. It is so bad that, even as she walks tall down the runway of life, the magnificent and glamour of her disappears at the mention of her status.

Her ability is undermined as she's seen *a labor with a kid not to talk of kids.* A pretty and working class 22 years old widow of a less than three year marriage stays widowed to her 30s. She is advised to settle for the available and leave her desire because the society has not done their duties in adding her to the social circles of acceptance as who she is not what she is. The most shameful act coming from women, who says God forbid, my son will not marry a widow, no matter how young, yet they give their daughter or support another young girl to marry a widower or a divorcee old enough to be her father.

The conspiracy of silence where, the society pretends a young widow in her twenties is celibate as the pastors preach holiness without remarriage of widows with the widows caught in the web is what we must begin to address. I strongly believe that teaching and preaching young widow's remarriage in our various cultural, social and religious environments will help our mental perception to be reoriented so that our young men will be attuned as their mothers though women like her learn to accept her with open arms. The men in their patriarchal attitude must begin to build the true value of women from their wives as they wear the daughters the gloves of strength to build their acceptance while raising our sons to be a Boaz; teaching then the value of her didn't less in her loss. And as women, we have to focus on the big picture as we leave the wall. It is our issue and together we will be able to build healthier practices for the happiness of another.

To the widows, we should learn to leave the wall of fears, focus on the big picture, and that is happiness. Find your purpose and explore your potentials. Create the posters of your desires and hang them on your emotional wall to admire, especially when widowhood paints its ugliest state, and fears flood in. This helps to overcome the unpleasant appearances of our culture as we work to raise a generation that will in principle build a society where women will not be labeled by the status of gender but by every right accrued to be fundamental in human need. The happiness of women did not end in the status of her marriage. For each one in widowhood, her joy is not a celebration of; all is well with his death, but a decision to evolve with the changing times that is life; as each step affirms a decision she made to begin again at his end hoping that it will be well. She is just learning that tides are season in the seasons, to which she must flow otherwise she'll be a stoppage for her generation that will steal their dream. Don't get lost in your loss, your happiness remains still in all abound.